# THE QUANTUM BLUEPRINT

# THE
# QUANTUM
# BLUEPRINT

ALIGN YOUR ENERGY.

UNLOCK YOUR POWER.

LEAD WITH PURPOSE.

SAMANTHA BALTADONIS

HOUNDSTOOTH
PRESS

COPYRIGHT © 2026 STRIVE SOLUTIONS HOLDINGS LLC
*All rights reserved.*

THE QUANTUM BLUEPRINT
*Align Your Energy. Unlock Your Power. Lead With Purpose.*

FIRST EDITION

ISBN   978-1-5445-5050-3  *Hardcover*
          978-1-5445-5049-7  *Paperback*
          978-1-5445-5051-0  *Ebook*

*Dedicated to*

*My baby, Oaklie Grace. My world, my everything. The reason I believe greater plans than ours exist. My courage. My conviction. My guiding light and my reason for believing life works out better than we could ever plan. May you live with the strength of a thousand lions and roar as softly as a lotus petal—always knowing your power, your worth, and your why.*

*My husband, Paul, the only person I've ever met who could pierce my exterior and match my inner intensity. You feed my brain and my soul—push me when I want fuel for growth, and comfort me when I need it most. Thank you for fanning my fire. I'm proud of who you are, who you're becoming, and who we've grown to be, together.*

*To Lisa Adnet, Coach Edwards, and Gary Keith, your wisdom was transformational in my life at critical points. I fear you don't know the weight of the blessing your presence carried. Thank you for leading with heart, giving me tough feedback, being a trusted advisor, and pushing me to pursue my full potential.*

*To the countless other teachers, mentors, and teammates I've encountered along this journey. Your time in my life, no matter how brief, is met with love and gratitude. If we were lessons for each other, may we part with any remaining residue, peacefully. If we orbited only distantly, know that your presence carries influence in the way you modeled empathy, courage, leadership—or taught me how to approach the absence of those qualities with more grace and patience.*

*This is for the ones rising, remembering, and reclaiming their power and their voice.*

# CONTENTS

INTRODUCTION .................................................................. 9
READING GUIDE ............................................................... 17
CARE WARNING ............................................................... 21

**PART ONE: ACTIVATION AND INQUIRY**
1. QUANTUM LEADERSHIP ............................................. 27
2. ENCODED FREQUENCIES ........................................... 49
3. FRAGMENTED LEADERS ............................................ 65
4. TUNING IN TO THE FIELD ......................................... 83
5. RECALIBRATING THE FIELD ..................................... 105
6. THE LEADERSHIP SHIFT .......................................... 123

**PART TWO: ALIGNMENT**
7. INNER AUTHORITY ................................................... 151
8. ENERGETIC INTELLIGENCE ...................................... 167
9. INTERPERSONAL ENERGETICS ................................ 185
10. ZERO-POINT ALIGNMENT ....................................... 207
11. TIDES OF TRANSFORMATION ................................. 223
12. QUANTUM STRATEGY ............................................. 239
13. ACTIVATING YOUR BLUEPRINT ............................. 257

AFTERWORD ...................................................................... 271
GLOSSARY ......................................................................... 273
RESOURCES ...................................................................... 279
NOTES ............................................................................... 285

# INTRODUCTION

> *"Ask not what your country can do for you; ask what you can do for your country."*
> —JOHN F. KENNEDY

We are standing at a crossroads—personally, collectively, and globally.

The world as we know it is shifting. Systems that have shaped society for centuries—economic, political, and social—are unraveling before our eyes. The structures we once relied on are proving unsustainable. Social division, environmental collapse, economic instability, and degrading trust in once unshakable institutions are not just random chaos; they are symptoms of an old system crumbling, making space for something new.

At this moment, we are being asked to make a choice.

Do we cling to outdated ways of being—cycles of fear, scarcity, and control? Or do we evolve forward? Do we allow power to consolidate into the hands of the few, or do we reclaim it as a collective force for transformation?

These choices have never been more urgent.

From the moment I realized my childhood was different from those around me, I longed to escape. I have learned to appreciate the difficult days just as much as the beautiful ones; both are necessary, part of the human experience. This book is a relic of my transformation journey—from poverty to rising corporate executive, and deciding to walk away from it all. It is inspired by my own pursuit of wholeness, the process of unlearning and relearning who I was and who I wanted to become, while navigating the world's expectations.

Along the way, I found something even more valuable: my purpose.

**MY WHY**

In *A Hidden Wholeness*, Parker Palmer perfectly describes the deep fragmentation many of us experience at some point in our lives: *the tragic gap*—the distance between who we are and who we want to be. He speaks to the gap between our inner truth and the external lives we build, aptly defining this as "a divided life." A life of contradiction and quiet suffering, living in silos where different parts of ourselves remain disconnected, unable to operate as a cohesive whole.

The philosophy underpinning this work draws from both ancient wisdom and modern organizational science: that true leadership is an act of becoming—aligning the inner and outer self so that our presence transforms the spaces we inhabit. It recognizes that leaders and systems should serve the employees, consumers, and communities who make their success possible. This is as much a quantum and spiritual practice as it is a strategic one.

We tell ourselves that we can be one person in our career and another in our personal life, that we can ignore our trauma and still function at peak performance, that we can move forward without having to contend with our past.

But when an event overwhelms our nervous system and exceeds our cognitive ability to process, it leads to suffering. Left unresolved, that trauma is magnified and compounds through other experiences in life, as messaging is reinforced or new pain is layered on.

There is no separation between who we are and how we lead. Our fragmentation eventually surfaces in the field—the environment we're in.

Your career thrives, but your relationships suffer. You pour into others, helping them heal, yet neglect wounds of your own. For a time, suppressing these tensions allows you to function, but eventually you pay with numbness, burnout, and an impending sense of doom, the feeling that no matter how much you achieve, something *still* isn't right.

**What we do with that tension shapes the reality we live in.**

Healing is more than repairing fragmentation; it is self-leadership and the daily intentional choice to live in alignment with who you truly are. First in our own lives, then in how we show up in our families, in our communities, and in service of the greater good.

My sense of purpose has not been fixed. It has shifted with roles, seasons, and challenges. At times, purpose meant survival. At other times, it meant growth, pushing the limits of possibility, or reimagining what it truly means to lead. Purpose, like leadership itself, evolves as we do—and this book invites you into that unfolding journey.

I grew up in poverty, raised by a meth-addicted mother. We moved often, but my worldview was shaped by rural blue-collar America.

The American Dream gave me hope when I had none.

I chose early on to live differently, to lead myself differently.

That internal resolve—fueled by a connection to something greater—a series of aligned moments, and relentlessly high standards for myself eventually led me to a decade-long career at

Amazon, where I led large-scale teams, guided multimillion-dollar transformations, and became known for my ability to turn chaos into strategy, and strategy into rapid results.

Through it all—early life and early career—my fascination with leadership never wavered.

What is leadership? What separates "good" leadership from "bad" leadership?

For most of my life, I thought leadership was about external validation: titles, influence, status. As I moved through my career, I realized leadership is about creating conditions where excellence and humanity can coexist. It is about embodying a presence that elevates others and calls forth their fullest potential.

**I now know that leadership begins with Inner Authority.**

Every leader carries the imprint of their past, shaped by internalized experiences, fears, and coping mechanisms that formed long before they ever stepped into a position of power.

I always knew my childhood was different from most. But I didn't realize how much I had blocked out to simply survive until the night when, at twenty-six, I had my first flashback. I woke to a scream that wasn't just mine. It belonged to the child I had once been. I sobbed for hours. It was one of the most vivid, physically painful, life-altering moments in my life. A full-body betrayal etched into my nervous system—undeniable.

My body remembered what my mind could no longer contain. In a single moment, everything I thought I knew shattered. I thought I had confronted the pain I carried from my childhood.

I barely started.

After that night, I set out on a mission to make sense of what I had experienced—to make sense of my story. A five-year intimate unraveling to understand what really happened to me.

*What else had I blocked out?*

I did my best, year by year, fleeting moment by fleeting moment. A brief scene here, a short and terrifying scene there. A few good moments sprinkled in between.

Moments of loss. Moments of survival. A flicker of terror, a fleeting moment of joy, then back into darkness.

I pieced together my past like fragments of shattered glass—some edges sharp, others softened by time. Memories are fickle when you're taught to doubt them.

As the pieces came together, deeper questions began to form.

Eventually, I stopped asking what happened to me and started asking why so few had escaped similar situations. Why do some people remain trapped in cycles of trauma, oppression, and limitation while others rise into wholeness, contribution, and purpose?

*Choice.*

A choice that has to be made over and over again—confronting hard truths, taking responsibility for our own patterns, recognizing that while our past may have shaped who we are today, it does not have to define who we become tomorrow.

## EVERY CHOICE WE MAKE IS EITHER A STEP TOWARD ALIGNMENT OR A STEP AWAY

In writing this book, I originally set out to simply tell my story. It seemed like the logical next step in my process—a way to share the wisdom gained from what I've lived through. As I began, I realized my story could not be told in isolation. This book became something much larger—a fusion of memoir, personal transformation, and leadership development.

A call to collective action, a movement, a soul-led revolution.

It is about the intentional work of becoming.

A lifelong process, one I cherish, one I hope to inspire others to embrace as well.

This book is about self-leadership and trusting your inner guidance. It's about moving through the world in a way that honors both your strength and sensitivity, your ability to create, and your ability to surrender. More than anything, it's about personal transformation in service of collective transformation. The responsibility we each have to heal, grow, and lead—not just ourselves, but through the collective shift that is already underway. If you're reading this, you have already begun.

This book describes how I began to shift from survival-based leadership to authentic alignment, and it's an invitation for you to do the same. This is about becoming fully yourself, then learning how to lead from that place—clear, connected, and aligned. It's about becoming someone who can hold power ethically, lead with resonance and coherence, and create safety in spaces too often defined by fear and domination.

My hope is that within these pages, you find the tools and inspiration to repair your own fragmentation and protective patterns, the strength to persevere and to step into the life you were always meant to lead. The way we care for ourselves, the habits we cultivate, the energy we allow into our space—and let influence our own—all contribute to how we show up in the world.

When we commit to healing and personal transformation, we embark on a journey of self-actualization—and *ideally*, self-transcendence. Through that process, we become the people we once needed.

We become the people the world is waiting for.

**Many believe leadership is external, measured by authority and action, but true leadership is deeply personal.**

As we learn to lead ourselves with integrity, in alignment with our purpose and in service of others, we influence our sphere—our portion of the world—and the collective continues to shift, gaining momentum with each person's progression from fragmentation back to inherent wholeness.

I have long wrestled with the discomfort of sharing my story, fearing that it would be mistaken as a plea for sympathy or an attempt to make it about me. This isn't about me.

This book—this journey, this message—is about you.

This book isn't meant to tell you who to be or what to believe. It's meant to remind you of the immense power of small choices, and to trust, to sense beyond what is immediately visible. It is an invitation to break free from survival patterns, from self-protection, learned helplessness, and the belief that someone else will come save you—a request to become deeply aware of who you are, to step into your highest potential, your truest self, and your unique purpose.

This book is a blueprint for reclaiming your energy, your impact, and *your role* in shaping what comes next. By the end, my hope is that you will understand, put into practice, and embody these principles.

**You will be the *proof* someone else needs.**

Proof that healing is possible, alignment is energetic, and leadership starts with the courage to transform *ourselves*.

This journey will challenge you. It will break you open. It will stretch you beyond what you thought possible. On the other side is a life of extraordinary freedom, alignment, and purpose.

The present moment demands something deeper than traditional leadership.

It demands people who have done the inner work. People who can lead themselves, regulate their emotions, manage their energy, embrace emergence, and create environments of mutual growth in relationships, workplaces, and communities.

**We need conscious, trauma-informed leaders.**

We need people who are mentally resilient, emotionally regulated, and energetically attuned. People who see through the illusion of separateness and recognize the real reason division is sown: to keep us from realizing our collective power.

The world doesn't need another surface-level self-help book. We need a mass awakening.

Trust the callings you receive. Follow your inner compass.

Even if something is not your final answer, it is *always* part of the path leading you forward.

Change starts within—*with you.*

I don't want you to read this and think, *Wow, she overcame so much.* I want you to read this and think, feel, and know: **I have everything I need within me to do the same.**

# READING GUIDE

Memories of my childhood don't come in order; they don't arrive neatly, in sequence, or chronologically. They were pieced together over years of reflection coming to me in flashes—visceral, sharp, and overlapping. Some are blurred, softened by time. Others are razor-sharp, etched into my body, mind, and soul.

They fracture, shuffle, and replay out of sync.

PTSD doesn't ask permission. It drags you, from scene to scene, with every *blink*.

Throughout this book, you'll notice those blinks: sudden shifts in time, memory, and sensation.

I have large memory gaps from age seven or eight, and everything from six to twelve is fuzzy. This is what my memory allows me to share. These moments aren't interruptions; they're illuminations, a glimpse into the unexpected jolts that occur in everyday life.

I include them to show you how fragmentation unexpectedly distorts safety, disrupts presence, and rewires perception. Tending to those wounds became part of my philosophy, and my understanding of leadership. Over time, learning to name and navigate those parts became the gateway to self-awareness, relational integrity, and leadership rooted in coherence—the alignment of one's internal state with external action, values, and purpose—expressed through relational presence rather than overt control.

Even now, "complete" feels like the wrong word. But I have made peace with what I know.

There are memories I will never get back. Some memories were stolen; others, I buried so deep I may never recover them.

But the ones that remain? They don't haunt me anymore.

**They stand as proof I survived. That I choose what comes next.**

Whether you're a leader in title or simply someone seeking fulfillment and greater impact, my hope is that you'll walk away from this book with a deeper understanding of yourself, and the courage to lead from the inside out. Collective progress depends on your leadership.

While healing is personal, it is never *only* personal. Each time one of us moves toward coherence, we subtly shift the collective field. Individual transformation strengthens collective consciousness, and collective consciousness, in turn, creates the conditions for deeper individual growth. This reciprocal loop positions personal alignment as the seed of systemic change.

*The Quantum Blueprint* offers a new lens for facilitating meaningful change—in life and leadership.

In the pages ahead, you'll discover the ability to sense, interpret, and direct the subtle currents shaping thoughts, emotions, and relationships—and how this becomes the foundation for Inner Authority, Energetic Intelligence, and Quantum Leadership.

This book is divided into two parts designed to reflect the personal transformation journey—recalibrating fragmentation into energetic alignment—then moving from survival to sovereignty. The first chapter is a high-level overview of the core ideas that will guide you through the rest of this book before we explore them in detail.

At the end of the book, reflective questions, or *Soulutions* (*soulutions*), are organized by chapter to assist you in navigating the path to unlocking your own blueprint and applying the tools and frameworks included in this book.

These questions are designed to evoke reflection, helping you integrate these concepts and reconnect with your own truth. In Chapter 10, the ALIGNED™ framework—a practical blueprint for transforming inner clarity into outward impact—is covered in depth.

Together, these elements connect personal transformation with regenerative systemic evolution—a shift critically needed across every sector and industry.

> New to any of these terms? I've included a glossary in the back of the book.

# CARE WARNING

This book contains vivid recollection of childhood trauma, neglect, and abuse.

Sharing my story is meant to empower, not re-traumatize.

Please read in a way that honors your well-being.

## BLINK

A dark bedroom, late at night. First, I see myself from above—I spend a moment observing the room. Window to the left, closet to the right, dim lighting from the bedside table lamp—and then suddenly I'm drawn back into my body. A palpable heaviness in my chest, jagged rock in my throat.

My whole body is weighed down by fear.

*I felt like I knew what was coming. Pretending to sleep didn't matter.*

He grabs my little waist. As I look up, he pulls me closer.

I'm overcome with sharp, shooting pain.

A bolt of lightning through my lower abdomen, yanking me from nightmare into vivid recollection—a secret so deeply buried—panting, screaming, sweating, sobbing, panic, confusion.

*Life was never the same after that.*

# PART ONE

# ACTIVATION AND INQUIRY

In 2017, after three years at Amazon, I was diagnosed with complex PTSD. At the time, I didn't have language for what was happening inside me—only the experience of flashbacks, hypervigilance, and the looming feeling that no amount of effort or healing was ever going to be enough.

While attempting to piece my trauma together and rebuild a life beyond the pain I had ignored for so long, I was working, leading, and navigating high-stakes environments where my internal state shaped *many* outcomes far more than I realized. I've spent much time reflecting on each role and experience, what I would have done differently in retrospect, and my own transformation.

What I've come to understand is that the patterns of fragmentation we carry within ourselves often perpetuate the dysfunction we see in organizations and systems. The beliefs, habits, fears, and self-doubt we carry silently shape our actions and behavior. When we begin to notice—to tune in to the signals of friction, exhaustion, or disconnection—we can choose a different response.

**Awareness leads to inquiry, inquiry to recalibration, and recalibration to alignment.**

Living in the tragic gap or enduring unresolved trauma fragments the self. Fragmentation creates internal and relational friction—especially under stress or change. In moments of friction, how we respond (with awareness or reactivity) reflects our development and alignment.

Part One invites you to notice and work with that gap—to repair, recalibrate—and step toward alignment. By exploring how encoded patterns influence us, we see how fragmentation shows up in leadership, and by tuning in to the field—the energetic environment we carry and contribute to—we reveal both the source of the problem and the beginning of the solution.

Our response to friction and misalignment is shaped by our self-awareness *and* the systemic forces we've internalized—

trauma, conditioning, power structures, cultural norms—and our capacity to regulate in real time.

Our response either fosters deeper connection and coherence, or reinforces misalignment and disconnection. Over time, these micro responses shape our leadership impact and ripple through our sphere of influence.

Our values, character, and sense of purpose all carry energetic frequency. They shift with our circumstances, but what matters most is whether they're aligned to our inner truth. Above all—living in alignment creates room for continual growth, assessment, and expansion.

# AWARENESS

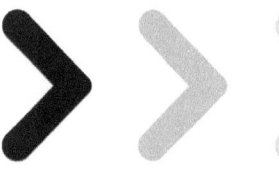

IDENTIFY UNACKNOWLEDGED DYSFUNCTION, PAIN POINTS, AND MENTAL MODELS

# 1

# QUANTUM LEADERSHIP

*"Never underestimate the magnitude of the power of the forces that reinforce the status quo."*
—JOHN P. KOTTER

Leadership is not *just* a role, a title, or one specific person. It is about the world we create within our sphere of influence, our energetic imprint on the ecosystem.

This occurs in families, communities, workplaces, and beyond—regardless of positional power.

Anywhere people interact, energetics are at play.

Quantum physics reveals that everything is energy—not just matter but vibration, potential, and interconnection—including our thoughts, emotions, and consciousness. Distinct from classical physics, which emphasizes linear cause and effect, quantum theory introduces principles like nonlocality (everything is connected), uncertainty (outcomes are shaped by observation and context), entanglement (individual parts influence the whole), and entrainment (the tendency of energies, rhythms, or systems to synchronize over time), suggesting our internal frequencies affect the environments we inhabit.

## LEADERSHIP IS THE SHIFT IN ENERGY, EXPECTATIONS, AND COLLECTIVE BEHAVIOR AS A RESULT OF YOUR PRESENCE

Not everyone considers themselves a leader. But whether we hold formal positions of power or not, we exist in the world *with* other people. Our presence naturally carries influence in the spaces we occupy; how we leverage this influence is the exercise of leadership.

My obsession with understanding "good" leadership began through early life experiences.

In first grade, my teacher selected me and another student to go to the library to research Martin Luther King Jr. for a classroom project. I was quiet and observant. That day, I felt seen. Trusted.

*Inspired.*

On another occasion, she gave me the opportunity to spell a word—*perseverance*—in front of the entire school. I still remember how it sounded, how heavy it felt, how proud I was.

She changed my perspective, and my life.

I didn't realize it then, but she was giving me more than a vocabulary word. She was speaking to my soul, initiating my mission—activating my Quantum Blueprint.

Perseverance became my anchor through an otherwise chaotic, confusing childhood.

Each experience I witnessed—mine or others'—became a data point to assess my reality and internal operating system through. A signal I'd use to inform my next move, initially a survival instinct, I learned to use it for protection, and then intentional expansion.

This early connection to what I now understand as Quantum

Intelligence—shaped by my upbringing and acute sensitivity—gave me the ability to sense hidden dynamics and navigate complex environments with clarity and discernment.

Eventually, on the rise from extreme poverty to corporate America, I had to learn how to navigate and influence the world as someone who feels deeply, reads between the lines, senses energy in a room, and anticipates unspoken tensions before they surface.

For a long time, I thought that sensitivity was a burden. Now, I recognize it as one of my greatest strengths and the basis of my leadership theory. This chapter offers a condensed thesis of the work ahead—so you can absorb the essence before we explore the practices, stories, and frameworks that bring change and transformation to life.

## PERSONAL TRANSFORMATION IS A LEADERSHIP IMPERATIVE

Quantum Leadership has been explored by a range of thinkers over the past few decades. I was first introduced to the concept during my graduate program at Gonzaga University while reading *Leadership and the New Science: Discovering Order in a Chaotic World* by Margaret J. Wheatley. She challenges traditional leadership paradigms by integrating quantum physics, chaos theory, and self-organizing systems. Positing that organizations function more like quantum fields—where energy dynamics, relationships, and emergent intelligence shape outcomes more than rigid hierarchies. She emphasizes that leadership is about fostering adaptability, trust, and decentralized decision-making—that organizations are living systems, not mechanical entities, and that leadership must shift to more fluid, responsive models.

In *Spiritual Capital: Wealth We Can Live By*, Danah Zohar and Ian Marshall introduce Quantum Leadership as a paradigm that integrates Spiritual Intelligence (SQ)—the capacity to act from deep meaning, ethics, and higher consciousness—with business strategy. They argue that SQ allows leaders to navigate uncertainty with coherence and trust, especially in volatile or emergent contexts.

More recently, Frederick Chavalit Tsao and Chris Laszlo have deepened this concept in *Quantum Leadership: New Consciousness in Business*, where they synthesize systems thinking, quantum science, and Eastern philosophy. Their approach advocates for a transformation in consciousness—from separateness to wholeness—as the basis for regenerative leadership.

Leadership is no longer strictly positional—it is energetic.

## THE FUTURE OF LEADERSHIP IS ABOUT CULTIVATING COHERENCE—WITHIN OURSELVES, OUR TEAMS, AND THE SYSTEMS WE MUST OPERATE IN.

Zohar and Marshall emphasize Spiritual Intelligence, Wheatley draws from systems science, and Tsao and Laszlo ground leadership in unity consciousness. **My work expands and integrates these threads to explore how energetics, power, and coherence interact in real time across people, teams, and systems**—turning alignment into an operational competency that shapes a leader's internal state and external impact.

This approach honors the wisdom of inner transformation and interconnectedness, while offering a grounded, trauma-informed, execution-focused path to restructuring power dynamics and embedding regenerative leadership at scale.

Leadership is an energetic exchange, a force that influences far beyond titles and hierarchy. When done with awareness, it creates expansion; when done unconsciously, it creates dysfunction.

Taking a trauma-informed, human-centered approach to leadership is not only the right thing to do; it aligns with Quantum

Leadership, complexity science, and living systems theory—where the leader's role is not to dictate but to *cultivate*.

Leaders who have done the inner work foster cultures of trust, resilience, and creativity—where people feel valued and empowered.[1] These environments provide the potential to elevate both the individual and the collective toward sustainable, interdependent growth.

Today, corporate culture rewards compliance and performance, often at the expense of humanity. Vulnerability is seen as a liability. Productivity is prioritized over well-being. DEI is being demonized. Belonging and psychological safety are treated as "nice-to-haves."

Leadership is primarily described in terms of execution, vision, and bottom-line results.

But beneath every decision, interaction, and dynamic within an organization, there are people. Those people bring everything with them: their experiences, their fears, and their survival mechanisms. Yet we act as if people can simply check their lives at the door—as if the unspoken weight of lived experiences don't shape how people lead and wield power.

While building my career and recovering from complex PTSD, I began to realize how deeply my energy, unprocessed trauma, and survival patterns shaped my leadership. This led me to question whether or not the majority of leaders have confronted their own fragmentation, the impact of this implication, and what leadership really means on a larger scale.

## QUANTUM LEADERSHIP IS REGENERATIVE PERSONAL AND COLLECTIVE TRANSFORMATION

Fragmentation—the gap between who we are and how we show up—affects decisions at every level, from menial interactions to systemic policies. Unresolved trauma in leadership often shows up as insecurity, emotional avoidance, or authoritarianism.[2]

Throughout this book, I propose that the healing journey—the process of repairing fragmentation from lived experiences that distort our inner truth—is conducted through a co-creative experiencing of life with conscious awareness.

This practice increases access to Energetic Intelligence, the ability to connect and move in alignment with the quantum field—the energetic data available in our environment. When we apply this process personally, we expedite transformation. When we apply it professionally, we can dissipate stagnation and amplify progression toward shared values and desired results.

My understanding of fragmentation, alignment, energetics—and their impact on organizational health and business results—laid the foundation for Quantum Strategy™, my approach to human-centered leadership and systemic transformation that integrates inner work with outer results. It is quantum—energetic and field based—grounded in principles we are still learning to understand as a society. While these concepts can feel complex, I invite you to connect with an open heart and trust the unseen forces that have always guided you.

After experiencing fragmentation in my core family unit for decades, then watching it play out across hundreds of people at Amazon in various positions of power, it clicked. Bypassing the pursuit of inner wholeness increases dysfunctional or abusive use of power and what is often described as the dark triad of leadership—narcissism, psychopathy, and Machiavellianism—resulting in self-serving behavior and collective regression.[3]

**Power without inner coherence distorts.**

It becomes a drug, a tool for numbing the wounds we've refused to acknowledge.

Like most people, I rose through the ranks by doing exactly what the system rewarded: delivering results and consistently outperforming expectations. At twenty-seven, despite my background and less than a 1 percent chance of rising to this level of "success," I had been promoted twice in three years. I was making six figures, and I was a "leader of leaders" responsible for the transformation of an organization of over three hundred people—at one of the largest tech companies in the world.

I felt like I "made it." By all external accounts, I was thriving. But underneath the facade, the mask, I was barely surviving.

To manage my internal chaos, I sought external control.

I resorted to what I had always done: building structure where there was none.

Over the span of eleven years—seven roles, nine teams, and eighteen managers—I was known for providing sound counsel, organizing chaos, delivering results, salvaging underperforming teams, and holding myself and everyone around me, including my leaders, to relentlessly high standards.

I could see threads no one else saw, and weave them into a clear path forward. I was the one people turned to when stakes were high, deadlines were tight, and failure wasn't an option. I received feedback like, "She's a fungible asset who can plug into any space and add immediate value" and "She sets a high bar for herself and others and consistently steps up when there are gaps." I was repeatedly described as a role model, trusted to dive deep, deliver results, and bring clarity to complexity.

Simultaneously, other colleagues said things like, "Sam brings strong energy and direction but occasionally overasserts" and "She makes it clear that the buck stops with her."

As I began defining my leadership style, I noticed it shifting under external expectations. Following increased organizational pressure to "raise the bar," I felt my soul split. Feedback was less about growth and more about urgency and optics. Instead of fostering collective growth and humanity, I began prioritizing patterns the system incentivized and rewarded. I was drifting further from the leader I wanted to be.

The feedback I received during this time reinforced this, praising my ability to drive results no matter the human cost. That was my wake-up call. The system was working as intended, and I had become complicit.

**I thought I made it, but "making it" in this environment demanded I constantly abandon myself.**

Leaders who rise without clear values, character, and ethics are more likely to crack under pressure and abide by unethical expectations. The boardroom becomes a battlefield, people are collateral, and personal accomplishments are a temporary salve for an internal void that we can never truly fulfill until we confront and address what's underneath.

I learned this most clearly during my time with FBA (Fulfillment by Amazon), leading a large team through two org-wide transformational initiatives. While feedback in my annual reviews praised my ability to "organize chaos," the traits I learned to rely on—urgency, pressure, perfectionism—the very strategies that helped me reach my current level of success, began holding me back. Patterns shaped by survival, slowly eroding my soul and my life force.

Eventually, burnout hit—emotional and physical exhaustion, depersonalization, and a profound sense of soul-level depletion.

At first, I thought it was imposter syndrome. But over time, I realized it was a normal response to an abnormal system—a system designed for performing and conquering, not healing, wholeness, or humanity.

**Burnout is a symptom of misaligned effort, energy, and focus.**

Misalignment occurs when our inner and outer realities conflict, often resulting in resistance, friction, communication breakdowns, fatigue, and burnout. It can show up organizationally as duplicated effort, stalled initiatives, or rising turnover, and personally as restlessness, emotional numbness, frustration with things that once brought joy, or the persistent feeling that something is missing.

Alternatively, alignment is the result of inner coherence, and vice versa. We experience congruence and clarity in our inner and outer worlds when our thoughts, emotions, and actions are in energetic integrity. Inner coherence *expresses outwardly*—actions, decisions, and energy matching your stated and espoused values.

You know when something feels off; actions, words, or presence betray your inner wisdom. The harder I pushed, the more fragmented I felt. My body was no longer just tired—it was signaling a profound misalignment. I couldn't out-strategize, out-hustle, or outrun the friction.

This way of living no longer aligned with the deeper call stirring in my heart. What had once protected and propelled me was now suffocating. I could no longer ignore the quiet truth rising within.

I fixed process after process, each with increasing complexity and impact. What I hadn't done—yet—was ask if the *way* I was leading was sustainable.

Or humane. Or healing.

It wasn't a strategy, commitment, or discipline problem; it was an energetic one.

I realized I was still operating from survival, thereby harming those I was accountable to, and undermining the legacy I wanted to create. I hadn't fully understood until then just how much unprocessed trauma shapes the way we show up in the world. To me, this revealed the limits of traditional leadership models and opened the door to explore more human-centered, transformational approaches—and then Quantum Leadership.

Frequency and vibration offer a valuable lens for leadership, revealing how the possibility of transformation increases when we intentionally live in alignment. This shift begins within, elevating our own state so that our leadership presence naturally lifts those we serve.

**Fragmentation doesn't go away in leadership—it shapes everything.**

Much of the feedback I received during those years felt off, filtered through other people's projections. Sanitized. Surface-level.

I wasn't being met in my frequency; I was being managed by theirs.

I realized feedback was rarely about me. It was about their nervous system's response to me.

The feedback I needed—the kind that speaks to expansion, growth, and true progress—wasn't going to come through formal channels.

Rather, it came through subtle signals—the way people pulled back or followed. And how I responded to them. I kept pushing through performance cycles and increasingly complex roles, consistently exceeding the bar in the ways the system demanded—but I knew something was off.

My nervous system knew.

What I experienced mirrored a larger systemic pattern: people burning out under systems that prioritize performance over all else. When people feel chronically depleted, their ability to meaningfully engage erodes. Toxic work environments—those that de-prioritize humanity—lead to higher turnover, lower engagement, and physical health consequences.[4] Leaders who burn out lose the ability to empathize because they're too focused on self-preservation, creating cultures of detachment and toxicity. When employees feel ineffective despite relentless effort, they disengage and stop creating, contributing, or imagining better ways forward.

Misalignment doesn't always look like exhaustion. Sometimes it shows up as feeling unfulfilled despite reaching a goal, "having it all" and still sensing an emptiness inside. The same frustrations, conflicts, and self-doubt resurfacing in different forms. These aren't signs of failure; they are signals of friction within people and the systems they serve.

When we pour energy into people, tasks, and systems that conflict with our values, we fragment—echoing fractures we've carried from early life experiences. These are invitations to look deeper, to examine what is unresolved, to stop suppressing and start integrating. If you find yourself wondering why joy feels fleeting, why you don't feel "enough," or why certain patterns keep cycling back, your inner world is asking for something more.

*Not more effort—alignment.*

## POWER IS NEITHER GOOD NOR BAD—IT IS SIMPLY A MAGNIFIER, REVEALING WHAT IS CURRENTLY UNDERNEATH

Leadership is an extension of identity, and identity is shaped by conditioning, survival mechanisms, and personal history. Unprocessed trauma, unresolved wounds, and unchecked ego do not disappear when someone steps into leadership. They become cracks in our character—influencing tendencies, relational patterns, and decision-making styles.

Industrial-era leadership models are built on ego. They reward dominance, competition, control, and external validation. As we explore what drives misalignment, it's important to clarify that ego itself is not inherently bad—it is just a messenger. Ego drives ambition, resilience, and self-actualization. Not all ambition or confidence is inherently destructive; the distinction is whether that ambition is rooted in alignment or avoidance. When left unchecked, ego becomes a fortress that blocks growth and connection; when integrated with discernment, it becomes a powerful ally in our evolution.

**The fragmentation of our true self is amplified when we're given power.**

Leaders who operate from fragmentation create environments of instability, distrust, and fear. An unhealed, fragmented leader wields power as a tool for control and dominance. A conscious leader channels power for transformation, trust, and evolution.

Traditional leadership relies on reward-and-punishment systems to drive performance, but this does not create transformational change or lasting success. Leaders who use external motivators—bonuses, penalties, or fear—may get compliance but never true commitment.

When people don't feel safe, they retreat. They withhold ideas, avoid challenges, and stay silent even when they know something isn't right. Sustainable motivation is rooted in autonomy (ownership), mastery (growth), and purpose (meaning). When given the choice, people don't leave bad jobs; they leave dysfunctional teams, systems, leaders, and cultures that fail to see them as human beings *first*. People thrive where they feel psychologically safe, seen, and supported.

Instead of shrinking under toxic leaders who mistake confidence for defiance, let's ask: how do I create a space where people feel safe enough to lead from radical responsibility rather than fear?

We can restructure teams, revise strategies, and launch change initiatives—but without transformation and alignment, these efforts risk re-creating the very dysfunction they were meant to dissolve.

*Transformation* has become the buzzword of modern leadership. But what does it actually mean or require?

Transformational leadership differentiates between transactional leadership built on exchange (do this, get that), and leadership built on vision (become, create).[5] When leaders inspire rather than demand, they build stronger, more resilient teams. Leadership that models emotional intelligence, well-being, and appreciative inquiry produces better outcomes than pressure-driven approaches.[6]

Transformational leaders do three things differently. They stimulate intellectual curiosity, encouraging new ideas rather than reinforcing old systems. They provide individualized support, seeing each person as more than just a role or function but as a human being with unique strengths and challenges. They lead with vision, creating a sense of purpose that moves people beyond their job descriptions.[7]

Some argue that transformational leadership is too idealistic, that in high-pressure environments, urgency must take priority over vision. Others suggest that pressure-driven leadership has its place in crisis management, when fast decisions and compliance are required. However, research suggests that even in high-stakes environments, fear-based leadership produces only short-term gains, often at the cost of long-term trust, innovation, and retention.

Without personal healing and alignment, these principles can still be co-opted by ego, urgency, or survival strategies.

Personal and collective transformation—and Quantum Leadership—begins with inner coherence: the alignment of energy, values, and actions with your purpose and the demands of the moment.

Whether leadership is expansive or constrictive has less to do with intelligence or credentials and everything to do with whether the leader has done their inner work.

Quantum Leadership shifts the conversation from *what leaders do* to *the energetic state they operate from*. While transformational models focus on vision and motivation, Quantum Leadership expands to the frequency beneath the behavior. Transformational leadership was a vital evolution—shifting us from control toward purpose and vision.

**Quantum Leadership invites us deeper—into who we are being and how our inner state shapes collective outcomes.**

In other words, it's not just about what you do but *who you are being while you do it*.

Personal transformation sharpens our awareness of energy—how it moves through us, how it informs our choices, and how it shapes the environments we lead. The more attuned we become to our internal signals, the more influence we have in shaping external impact.

**Leadership that transforms starts within.**

David R. Hawkins's *The Map of Consciousness Explained* offers a calibrated scale of emotional and energetic frequencies—from shame and guilt to love, joy, and enlightenment. His work asserts that every emotional state carries a measurable vibrational frequency—and that individual and collective transformation occurs as we shift from low-frequency (contractive, fear-based) states to high-frequency (expansive, love-based) states.

Ultimately, how you interpret, communicate, and use your inner energy shapes not only the spaces you influence but the means, methods, and motivation underlying your pursuit of collective and personal transformation.

Leadership that minimizes harm and maximizes human potential creates the conditions for individuals and communities to co-create, progress, and thrive together.

Conscious leaders cultivate trust, while fear-driven leaders cultivate control.

**The systems we live and work in are misaligned because we exist in and lead from fragmentation.**

Mind from body, strategy from soul, and presence from power. We've inherited models that reward productivity over purpose, and performance over coherence.

$$\text{Change} \neq \text{transformation}$$

$$\text{Transformation} \neq \text{alignment}$$

But alignment unlocks transformation that actually sticks and scales.

Most people don't associate trauma and leadership. Even fewer recognize that a leader's unhealed fragmentation shapes the entire ecosystem around them. This is a critical opportunity—a strategic advantage—and an invitation to transformational growth. When leaders take responsibility for their own energy, they model a new way forward, breaking cycles of dysfunction within their sphere of influence. Healing isn't separate from leadership; it is the foundation of it.

Personal transformation isn't just personal—it's organizational, relational, and systemic. This is a way of being, a *blueprint* to collapse barriers, dissolve distortion, and lead from possibility.

## TRANSFORMATIONAL LEADERS CHANGE WHAT WE DO—QUANTUM LEADERS TRANSFORM WHO WE ARE

In many ways, Quantum Leadership is the deep inner change that transformational leadership theory originally pointed toward, but often gets lost in systems that prioritize output over alignment. It expands transformational principles by asking not just how we grow, but from what level of consciousness and in pursuit of what outcome, inviting us to consider the state of awareness shaping our actions—our level of personal integration and what is being called forth within the systems we operate.

**Transformational leadership demonstrates how we *change things*—Quantum Leadership provides the blueprint to how we *change ourselves.***

While research already points to psychological safety, trust, emotional intelligence, and nervous system regulation as essential to effective leadership, Quantum Leadership integrates and expands on these through the lens of Energetic Intelligence—revealing the unseen forces that shape behavior, decisions, and systemic outcomes.

**Energy cannot be destroyed, only transformed.**

Energetic Intelligence (EnQ) is the ability to sense and interpret the energetic undercurrents—to discern whether actions stem from grounded intention or from stress, fear, or unresolved patterns.[8] EnQ moves leaders beyond surface-level observation into attunement with the forces influencing individual and collective dynamics in real time. From that awareness, they invite grounded, growth-oriented dialogue that re-centers safety and supports aligned momentum.

While others have explored Energetic Intelligence in different contexts, my application in the realm of Quantum Leadership focuses on how leaders detect, interpret, and respond to the energetic patterns beneath behavior—integrating self-awareness and attunement to the environment and field with discernment—turning subtle cues into strategic and systemic insight.

Leadership, at its core, carries a profound responsibility to nurture, not diminish, the human spirit. When leaders operate from unresolved fragmentation and misaligned ego, when internal misalignment goes unchecked, even our best intentions manifest as harm or dysfunction. To usher in the next era of leadership, we must transcend egocentric, control-based systems and embody Quantum Leadership—for ourselves and the spaces we influence. It is time to stop forcing agendas that serve the few, and shift instead toward strategies that uplift the whole.

The future of leadership is not about singular authority. It's about emergent intelligence—where adaptive, aligned groups drive systemic transformation through co-creation, the development of a shared vision, and limited centralized control. I'm not suggesting we do away with hierarchy. I'm suggesting, rather, that people with positional power develop cultures that support emergent, co-creative solutions toward a specific outcome without bogging down the team with their own fear and fragmentation.

Quantum Leaders understand that accountability without safety breeds fear, while safety without accountability leads to stagnation. The goal is to create high-trust, high-performance environments where individuals feel safe enough to take risks; to give and receive constructive insight about their impact; and to push themselves to grow—without fearing punishment or rejection.

The future of leadership—whether business, politics, or personal—depends on our ability to heal, integrate, and lead from a place of radical wholeness. When people and leaders are internally misaligned, it energetically reverberates through team dynamics, decision-making, and culture. Without first checking alignment within ourselves, we won't recognize misalignment in others or in the systems we lead. The shift from fear-based leadership to conscious leadership begins with internal transformation—closing the gap between who we are internally and how we lead externally.

**True leadership begins with personal accountability. It's not about how well you lead others. How well do you lead yourself?**

Energetic Intelligence, personal transformation and alignment allow us to lead in complex environments without collapsing into fear, avoidance, or overcompensation. Leaders who integrate inner work into their growth strengthen emotional intelligence, navigate conflict with clarity, and inspire through presence rather than force.

Quantum Leadership is rooted in energetic coherence—how individual and collective energy patterns shape the behaviors, decisions, and dynamics that reinforce existing systems or catalyze meaningful transformation.

**Leadership is about who we are beneath the role and title.**

The question is not whether past wounds influence leadership; it is whether we will allow them to subconsciously dictate our future, or choose to lead intentionally, from a place of integrity and inner alignment. You don't need a team to be a leader. You need clarity, coherence, and Inner Authority.

As the world and leadership continue to evolve, we're being called to move beyond hierarchical, industrial-era leadership models that erode psychological safety, and instead foster systems of shared responsibility, adaptability, and relational growth. The most effective leaders will be those who lead from Inner Authority—a cultivated sense of self-trust and discernment rather than fragmentation.

When we lead without healing, we project our wounds onto those we serve.

When we lead with awareness, we create spaces where others can rise.

Quantum Leaders cultivate energy, presence, and the pursuit of collective benefit alongside profit by aligning their internal signal with external impact—creating a field of coherence, where personal and energetic alignment propel individual and collective transformation.

**Leadership is the energetic imprint you leave on people, planet, and progress.**

**BLINK**

Two, maybe. A one-bedroom, one-bath cabin sitting atop a snowy hill, tucked near the forest of a small town in Eastern Washington. Dark brown, grayish exterior, a tall chimney. Smoke billowing from it. Kettle Falls, Washington, population 1,200, maybe less.

*I don't remember much from my mother's first marriage. I think this was before my baby brother was born. My life takes some interesting turns between 1992 and 2002, the next time we would return to Kettle Falls.*

**BLINK**

Three? Four? Single-story apartment building for a brief period of time.

*This is where I was kidnapped, or so the story goes.*

*My mom claims that when she was going through the divorce from her first husband, my brother's father, he and his family wanted to take me and my brother from her.*

*Allegedly, her ex-husband broke in and kidnapped us in the middle of the night from that apartment.*

*This might explain my inability to sleep alone, or to live on the first floor of an apartment building. Otherwise, I have no memory of any of it. And if this did happen, I have no idea how I ended up back with her.*

**BLINK**

A large, white, multiunit building up on a hill. Second or third floor. Mom is working; I am going to school through Head Start.

*Life feels relatively "normal" when I look back on this time.*

*Funny. She always said, "normal is just a setting on a dryer."*

*Justification for smoking meth on a random Tuesday—maybe. Actually, I do have joy associated with this place, these memories. A rarity, so I try to hang on to them.*

I can see her smile from the kitchen, making food for my brother and me while we sing the clean-up song from *Barney & Friends*. She is a trained cosmetologist, but eventually starts working in jewelry design—a job she loves, something she is proud of.

To this day, it brings tears to my eyes. *She was doing it. She was figuring it out.*

*What happened? What went wrong?*

### BLINK

Four? Five? Standing on a busy downtown street with a distinct rounded corner—*a tall beige building behind her*—my mom kneels down in front of me. She looks me straight in the eyes with fear and emphatically stresses, "*you* cannot tell them anything, or they will take you from *me!*"

*This was one of the few memories of my childhood that stood out, a nagging mystery. I always thought it was odd. Why this particular memory? Something about it must be significant.*

*Thirty-plus years later, I'd know why. It was the first time I can remember internalizing the "good girl" mentality—suffocating truth for the comfort of others' mediocrity.*

"Be a good girl."

"Do as I say, not as I do."

"What happens in this house stays in this house!"

*At that young of an age, you obey. You do as you're told, especially by your mother. She's meant to protect me. Right...*

*Right?*

### BLINK

Six years old, I think. My baby sister was recently born, so by now I've experienced and witnessed my mother's parenting style enough for my little brain to begin internalizing her approach. I'm playing with my baby dolls.

"Be good!" I yell, and then spank my doll before putting it into the baby swing or stroller. As I scold my baby, my mom walks around the corner. I turn to meet her eyes and see *concern*, an unusual softness. "Do you talk to your baby like that because that's how I talk to you and your brother?"

*I think that was the first time my little brain and heart registered that there was another way to be a mom.*

*I wanted to be a "good" mom.*

*I began to recognize "bad" mom qualities in her.*

*Throughout my most formative years, I was referred to by the broader family as "the mother hen." I didn't realize I was going to be mothering my mother too. Did they?*

# ENCODED FREQUENCIES

*"Until you make the unconscious conscious, it will direct your life and you will call it fate."*

—CARL JUNG

Who we become as parents, mentors, decision-makers, and leaders is not separate from who we were taught to be as children. Our default leadership style is shaped by what we learned was acceptable, what we feared, and what we believed about power, control, and our own worth.

My first model of leadership—the original blueprint for how I navigated power, pain, and personal responsibility—was handed down through generations of unhealed trauma and survival-based choices. My story illustrates the very patterns so many of us unconsciously re-create.

**Encoded frequencies—the unconscious beliefs and behaviors we inherit—silently shape our personal lives, our relationships, and the systems we exist within.**

Trauma occurs when something overwhelms you, or when it

gets processed through a distorted lens—one that doesn't resonate with your soul but was imprinted by your environment or early conditioning. When we can't make meaning in a way that aligns with our truth, we fragment. This applies to any experience, acute or cumulative, that exceeds your capacity to process or make meaning in real time. Parts of us go offline in an effort to be accepted, or to survive.

Fragmentation is the imprint of that adaptation. It embeds itself in the body and psyche, creating energetic imprints that shape our beliefs, behaviors, relationships, and leadership styles. It becomes a background operating system that runs silently—until we bring it into awareness.

## LEADERSHIP IS WHO WE ARE AT OUR CORE AND HOW WE SHOW UP IN THE WORLD

I was born in Spokane, Washington, in 1990 to a single mother, just barely out of her teens. She had my brother less than two years later and married his father. He would be the first of a series of men to come in and out of my life, each disruptive and dangerous in their own way. At the time, she was a trained cosmetologist and had been living the high life (literally) long before I came along.

In the early years, her drugs of choice were alcohol and cocaine. By the mid-1990s, she upgraded to meth. Her other drug of choice was men, preferably abusive and unfaithful.

Some sort of generational curse. A continuation of the same cycle she grew up in. The legacy of unresolved pain moved from one generation to the next, unspoken.

From what I understand about my family history, my grandmother—pregnant at seventeen in the early '70s—was kicked out of her home and disowned for bringing shame to the family.

That kind of rejection leaves a lasting mark.

She moved in with her boyfriend, and they had a second child, a son, within two years. My grandfather became an abusive alcoholic; eventually my grandmother found the resources and resolve to leave. As a single mother of two, with no access to safe, reliable childcare, she relied on a neighbor to care for her two young children. Many of us know where the story goes from here. The babysitter's son stole my mother's innocence—one choice echoed across generations—shaping everything that followed.

He didn't only cause pain for her, in that moment.

It reverberated through the rest of her life, as it does for most survivors.

The guilt. The shame. The erosion of a belief in inherent self-worth.

I wouldn't fully understand the depths of her unhealed trauma until much later in my healing journey. She followed the same cycle her mother did. Marrying an abusive man. Having children too young. Finding solace in substances that dulled the pain.

Addiction has a way of swallowing people whole. Food. Drugs. Work. No matter the numbing agent, it leaves a void that nothing can fix—no matter how hard you try.

She went to rehab, at least twice that I recall. But rehab doesn't work if you don't want it to.

She was *so* good at pretending. She could make herself seem like a functioning adult long enough to fool landlords, employers, even social workers. But behind closed doors, I carried it all—the worry, the responsibility, the fear—stepping into roles no child should, constantly on guard and on edge. I hated her for a long time. I still do, some days. It's hard not to when the very person meant to care for, provide for, and protect you causes you the most harm.

**If we don't examine our encoded frequencies, we repeat them.**

For years, I struggled with emotions that did not feel like mine. The weight of anxiety, fear, and hypervigilance existed before I had words for them. The way my body tensed in certain situations, the way my mind scanned for danger, even in safe places. I thought it was just who I was.

When something is all you've ever known—whether it's emotional suppression, chaos, or control—it doesn't feel wrong. It just feels like life. I knew, as a young girl, that if I wanted a different life than the one I was born into, I had to make different choices. And, to fulfill my purpose, I had to heal.

I began to question my environment, my upbringing, and what I was unconsciously carrying forward.

At the core of intergenerational trauma is unfinished emotional processing. When trauma isn't fully acknowledged or healed, its effects don't simply disappear; they become embedded in family narratives, behaviors, and even biology. Some wounds do not begin with us, but they live within.

They may not be ours to carry, but we still bear their weight, and they become ours to heal.

From the moment we are born, we inherit more than just genetics; we inherit ways of existing in the world. Some of these inheritances serve us, while others keep us trapped in cycles we never consciously agreed to. Trauma doesn't end with the person who first experiences it. It often ripples through generations, shaping behaviors, beliefs, and even biology. Even without direct experience, we may carry the emotional imprints of past generations.

Research in epigenetics has shown that generational trauma alters gene expression, affecting how descendants process stress, fear, and resilience.[9] Intergenerational trauma exists and operates on a biological and emotional level, while behavioral conditioning works through direct experience and reinforcement. This further explains why we unconsciously replicate the habits, fears, and emotional responses of those around us, even if we don't consciously agree with them.

For a long time, I thought trauma lived only in memories. But it lives in reactions—in the tension you carry into conversations, in the control you bring to your team, in the way your body braces before you speak. Trauma gets trapped in the nervous system when a survival response (fight, flight, freeze, or fawn) is interrupted.[10] If left unresolved, it keeps us locked in reactive cycles, reinforcing subconscious programming, repeating the same patterns over and over again.

This is why children of abusive parents struggle with regulating their own emotions, or children of emotionally unavailable caregivers find themselves in relationships where they feel unseen, or trauma survivors become overachievers, seeking control where they once felt powerless.

Consistent exposure to trauma overwhelms the nervous system, disrupting emotional regulation and making trust and connection harder to access. Early trauma rewires the brain's stress response system, making stress feel like a baseline state, making it feel *normal*.

Growing up in chaos, you learn to adapt. And that's what I did.

During critical developmental periods, while other kids were learning how to express emotions openly, navigate friendships, and communicate their needs, I was learning how to read subtle energy, and sense unspoken shifts in mood—to decode power dynamics and adjust my behavior accordingly.

I wasn't just learning how to survive; I was learning how to anticipate the need for survival before a threat even arrived—to control my environment. I learned how to read people, how to spot danger before it reached me. I learned how to stay invisible when necessary and how to be noticed when it served me. I learned how to make a plan, execute it, and not rely on anyone else. Those skills worked really well for me, until they didn't.

Eventually, it kept me from truly living, connecting, or leading with openness.

Without realizing it, I fell behind in developing traditionally understood and accepted communication and engagement skills that define connection in modern society. I began to see how trauma showed up as overfunctioning and taking on more responsibility than I should. The same adaptation skills that once protected me and helped me reach certain levels of success became barriers to the very expansion and alignment I was striving for. What once kept me safe later manifested as control, emotional detachment, and an inability to trust; my hypervigilance, independence, and the ability to assess possible threats prevented deeper growth, connection, and fulfillment.

Every structure I built to protect myself—my identity, success, and strength—was tested, challenged, and, in many ways, destroyed. At first, I resisted. I intellectualized my healing, trying to outthink my wounds instead of feeling them. I chased achievements, believing that external validation could replace internal sovereignty.

Exposure to trauma is not something we can control, but we can control our response to it. We are capable of integrating our experiences so we can live and lead from our authentic blueprint—even in the midst of chaos and uncertainty.

Whether it's our own experience or intergenerational trauma or both, unhealed trauma sits deep within us, playing itself out again and again. It repeats. It shows up in our relationships, our parenting, our daily choices, affecting our ability to love, to trust, to regulate, and to lead.

By fifteen, I was beginning to repeat inherited patterns, running from my pain in all the wrong ways. At nineteen, I naively made the decision to start a family with a man who, in reality, was deeply unprepared to be a partner or father. I didn't realize then that I was repeating a familiar cycle, one I had absorbed from my own upbringing—staying in unhealthy dynamics, mistaking struggle for commitment, and believing I could "fix" someone else's pain.

Healing isn't a gentle unfolding; it's a dismantling. A forced reckoning. Quantum Intelligence will *always* give you the opportunity to evolve, but if you resist, it will find another way to break you open.

Your past does not have to define your future.

Childhood adversity research found that trauma-informed care and early intervention can significantly improve outcomes, proving that resilience can be built.[11] Not every child with a high ACE (adverse childhood experience) score is destined for dysfunction. Many go on to lead stable, thriving lives. Early nurturing, strong social bonds, and emotional repair reshape stress response, increasing adaptability and regulation. Trauma *and* healing can alter gene expression.[12] Practices like somatic therapy, meditation, and intentional emotional processing don't just shift our mindset—they literally rewire the brain.[13]

Healing is emotional *and* biological.

Post-traumatic growth research suggests that adversity can serve as a catalyst for transformation when paired with self-awareness, resilience, and meaningful relationships.[14]

For years, I wrestled with my past, trying to make sense of what had happened to me, why I reacted the way I did, and whether my memories were reliable. I needed to know why my responses to pain had once been valuable survival mechanisms but were now barriers to continued success. I needed to understand why my body held so much tension, why I lived in a constant state of hyperawareness, why my mind constantly replayed the past.

Flashbacks started pulling memories from the shadows of my mind, forcing me to sit with things I had long buried. But I didn't trust myself, not fully. I needed proof. I needed something tangible to validate what I had always known.

Healing, at first, felt like a mystery I could unravel only if I had all the facts. I went to my mother first. But asking her for the truth was like asking a compulsive liar to suddenly develop a conscience. The truth wasn't something she wouldn't give me—it was something she simply couldn't.

She had rewritten history so many times that she had convinced herself it was real. So I turned to the one place where lies couldn't erase the past. I requested my case files from the state, thinking they would provide clarity—answers—a definitive account that would validate my experience.

Deep down, I already knew.

**My body had been telling me the truth long before any document could confirm it.**

Proof became my obsession. I didn't doubt my own experiences, but I needed a reality no one could deny. In mid-2021, I received confirmation of what I had always known. The very first entry in my file described visible injuries and words I had spoken as a child.

In a single paragraph: evidence of what my body and soul had been telling me for decades.

My mother, caught up in a divorce, dismissed it as fiction, as manipulation, as something too inconvenient to be real.

That moment on the corner of a busy downtown street when she told me I couldn't tell. The psychiatrist's office. The bedroom it occurred in, the lamp on the table next to my bed, casting a golden hue.

I finally understood how it all connected.

For thirty years, I lived with the weight of that dismissal.

The gaslighting. The doubt. I knew the truth all along, but for the first time in my life, I had proof.

*"She has an appointment at the deaconess abuse center to have her daughter [interviewed] on 4/5/94 and was told to make cps report."*

I was three years and three months old.

Among the records, a note from a few years later when I was in first grade—a case worker visited my elementary school after numerous failed attempts to reach me at my home address: *"I spoke with her in the principal's office w/the principal present. I questioned her about her mother and home life. Samantha usually nodded, or said yes or no, not offering much dialog about what goes on at home. She didn't indicate that there was anything out of the ordinary at home.* ***Her mother mentioned the first time I talked with her that I could interview her children but they wouldn't tell me anything.****"*

That validation gave me something I had been missing for decades: self-trust. When you grow up in an environment of denial, dismissal, and manipulation, you learn to question your own reality.

Reading those files was like reclaiming a piece of myself that had been denied for thirty years.

That was the foundation I needed to begin again, to close that book and begin writing a new story. After decades watching my mom suffer, many times caught in the grip of her own mind, I learned the importance of the stories we tell ourselves, and how they shape our identity.

Through my own suffering, I learned they also hold the key to our healing.

## LEADERSHIP ISN'T RESERVED FOR BUSINESS—IT'S THE STORY WE TELL OURSELVES ABOUT WHO WE ARE AND WHO WE'RE CAPABLE OF BECOMING

Trauma is not just something that happens to us. It's something we carry, respond to, and unconsciously operate from. These aren't just personal wounds—they become leadership patterns, shaping how we hold power, make decisions, and treat others.

Before we can lead others with integrity, we must first reclaim the narrative that shapes our own identity and experiences. The journey can be brutal at times. You will question everything: who you are, what you believe, whether you're even capable of transforming. But eventually, something shifts. The weight lifts. The patterns break. You realize that the version of yourself you fought to protect was never meant to be permanent.

You were always meant to evolve, to transform.

**Our past does not define us; it informs the power we hold to shape our future.**

As I finally began to unravel and reclaim my story, I found myself returning to my mother's story. I have compassion for the teenager who had a child in 1970, only to be cast out by her parents, abused by her boyfriend, and left to survive on her own. Out of desperation, she trusted a neighbor to watch her daughter, unknowingly placing her in harm's way. The guilt of that decision shaped the rest of her life, turning motherhood into a cycle of rescue rather than responsibility.

In trying to atone, my grandmother enabled more than she protected—funding my mother's addiction, bailing her out of jail, and providing a home without accountability. Her love, tangled with regret, kept my mother trapped in victimhood, always waiting to be saved.

I can have compassion for their suffering without excusing the impact it had.

Looking back now, I understand what she meant when she asked if I spoke to my dolls the way she spoke to me. It was the first time she saw herself in a mirror she couldn't ignore. Maybe, for just a moment, she realized what she was creating.

I wish that realization had been enough.

I wonder what her life would have been like, had she had the strength to confront her own pain, and to heal—if she had been willing to sit in the discomfort, to face the darkest parts of herself.

**The weight of our stories is undeniable, but we decide how to carry them.**

The only real choice we have is whether we initiate that transformation ourselves, or wait until life forces it upon us. I chose both, at different times. When I finally surrendered to the unraveling, I stopped *barely surviving* and started *intentionally becoming*.

For years, I thought "healing" was the finish line, a point where resilience and success converged into stability. But lasting transformation isn't just about arriving at a place of self-awareness; it's about what we do with it. Healing is breaking cycles, leading with integrity, and stepping into the fullest, most aligned version of yourself.

It is reclaiming the power to shape our own narrative—seeing ourselves as architects of our future rather than products of our past.

**Self-leadership is not about erasing what happened; it's about shifting the way it lives within you.**

Transformation begins when we stop asking, *what happened,* and start asking, *who do I choose to become despite what happened?*

### BLINK

Five? Six? My little brother, my mom, and I are living in a house in Spokane with my mom's new boyfriend. There's a basement. The church kitty-corner across the street. Detached garage in the back. And milk. Milk in the fridge. Odd detail. He will become the father to my mother's third child, my baby sister, born in April of '96.

*I don't really know how we ended up there. My memory flashes between a duplex, the apartment on the hill, and this house. I don't have memories of my mother being pregnant.*

### BLINK

Wait, there's another house. Large bushes in the backyard. A separate garage. The one where my brother finds a grenade in the backyard and SWAT shows up.

*Or is that just what she told me?*

### BLINK

Six? Seven? My mom, brother, and I are flying to Seattle. She has introduced us to another guy, a rocker, painter.

*Think 1990s version of* Breaking Bad *meets* Sons of Anarchy.

Long, red hair; tattoos. Cool dude, but things start to get weird when he shows up. Faint memories of an A-frame cabin. Him and his "band" are playing rock music downstairs. My brother and I are upstairs.

*We ended up catching chicken pox or something.*

*I'm fairly confident this is when my mom's drug of choice changed from alcohol and cocaine to meth. And when I started to realize I was living a very different life than most kids.*

## BLINK

Seven. White house. Same block my uncle, great uncle, and great-grandparents live on.

*The first time I felt the pain of hunger was in that house. I learned to take care of myself in that house, still a kid myself.*

Summer '98. I want to go get milk for cereal. I grab some money, hop on my bike, and start pedaling down the alley toward the corner store. About halfway down the block, I notice that one of my friend's dogs is wrapped around the trampoline, unable to get to his water. I untangle him and walk across the yard to pet their other dog. As I put my hand on his head, he lunges at me, biting my face at least twice—once around my left eye and once on my cheek and chin.

I run home. A cold sensation drips down my face.

I run through the back door, and in slow motion, my mom turns around, screams, drops the phone, grabs a towel, puts it on my face, and rushes me to the car.

*I don't remember screaming or crying, just the taste of the blood.*

I want to see so badly. I keep trying to flip the visor down to look. My mom keeps flipping it back up, telling me that I cannot. She races to the emergency room, we go in, and a screech immediately pierces the air. A woman turns and runs the other way. I'm rushed back to an operating room by an entourage.

*The fear in other people's eyes is what got me. I had no idea how bad it was until I saw the way everyone looked at me. Terror and genuine fear in their eyes.*

I was bit by a bullmastiff, an enormously large breed of dogs that are highly protective. I was in surgery for twelve-plus hours and had to have over one hundred stitches.

I remember feeling like I was in trouble—covering for the dog, like I had learned how to cover for my mom. To "take my mind off of it," my mom and her boyfriend said we would go on a cross-country road trip.

We drive from Spokane to Wyoming and camp in the Pathfinder along the way.

After this trip, mom tells me we're moving to Seattle, "to a mansion! It's going to be amazing! We're starting a whole new life."

# LEADERSHIP

ASSESS INFLUENCE, ACCOUNTABILITY, AND ENERGETIC PRESENCE

# FRAGMENTED LEADERS

*"Listening moves us closer, it helps us become more whole, more healthy, more holy. Not listening creates fragmentation, and fragmentation is the root of all suffering."*
—MARGARET J. WHEATLEY

After more than a decade of deep leadership research, including eleven years at Amazon, I've seen the same invisible root cause emerge across every system: misalignment, stemming from individual fragmentation, is the silent root cause of organizational dysfunction, burnout, and underperformance. Until we address this, even the most well-structured, well-intentioned strategies will struggle to take root.

Neuroscience shows that trauma imprints survival strategies into the brain's circuitry, and neuropsychology confirms that these strategies—whether overfunctioning to prove worth or self-sabotaging to avoid risk—can become unconscious defaults. When wounds go unexamined, they rewire the nervous system and reshape the mind.

In quantum terms, repeating the same behavior over and over is like collapsing into a single probability state and cutting yourself off from the full field of possibility—rather than accessing it through coherence and alignment. Over time, these responses harden into personality or are written off as "just my style," creating a self-imposed glass ceiling that limits potential. Unless we intentionally navigate these patterns, they become the lens through which we lead.

Fragmented leadership isn't always loud or dysfunctional. Sometimes it hides behind ambition, achievement, or "success"—seeking external validation in the form of titles, money, and recognition because we fear addressing an inner disconnect.

I stayed at Amazon longer than intended. Originally, my plan was to leave after five years to become a coach, an author, and to pursue my PhD. But ego, financial security, and a sense of proving myself kept me there for over a decade. I became attached to the success story—the idea that I "made it" after coming from nothing, and that this somehow proved my worth.

This attachment blinded me to the fact that I had outgrown the environment and was delaying stepping fully into my purpose. Reflecting on my career so far, I noticed that despite my consistency in manner, tone, and presence, my passion has been received in dramatically different ways. Some saw it as a catalyst and leaned in with excitement; others, feeling threatened or unsettled, tried to contain or diminish it.

**What we don't heal, we re-create. Nowhere is that more visible than in leadership.**

When we lead from unhealed wounds, we become attached to misaligned paths that reinforce our fragmentation. While many leaders often saw me as committed, highly effective, and results-driven, others offered *superficial* perspectives: *Smile more. Wear less makeup. You're too stoic; try to be more approachable.*

You're intimidating.

That last one stung particularly bad. It was one of those

that had been repeating in my mind for decades. Every time I demanded better leadership from my mother, she'd say, "You're so intimidating! Not everyone has a good head on their shoulders, Samantha."

Excuses. Insults to make me uncomfortable for pointing out her inadequacies.

## LEADERSHIP IS A REFLECTION OF WHO WE ARE AND WHAT WE HAVE—OR HAVE NOT—HEALED

I fundamentally believe very few people exist in the world intentionally trying to harm others; most people I crossed paths with were doing their best. Yet there were times I felt the quiet dissonance of choices that didn't align with integrity—when words and actions didn't fully match. Even when I assumed positive intent, my body registered friction in the gap between stated values and actual behavior.

That gap became its own kind of initiation, testing whether I would acclimate to the system or stand apart from it.

Over time, I saw how some people learned to align with existing power structures, becoming gatekeepers of the very dynamics they once sought to transcend. What felt personal was actually systemic. These patterns aren't unique; they show up across leaders and industries.

My story isn't unique—it is a microcosm of what plays out every day in boardrooms, organizations, teams, and families led by fragmented leaders. Many high-achieving individuals stay trapped in cycles of overworking, perfectionism, and people-pleasing, believing that if they can just work harder, they will feel *enough*.

Self-leadership is the foundation of personal transformation. It is the ability to influence and direct your thoughts, actions, and energy to intentionally live in alignment.

I found myself ruminating: *were they seeing something I couldn't or were they projecting their own survival strategies and discomfort onto me?* Relational dynamics reveal patterns that build tension or invite expansion—both offer an opportunity for growth when viewed through a quantum lens.

These weren't bad people. They were running a script. And for a while, so was I.

As my healing deepened, I started to notice the same pattern in every space I entered. The more whole, confident, and internally powerful I felt, the more I began to activate others. During one meeting, while I was pushing back on strategic failure points they didn't want to deal with, one director said, "Can you just stop? You're not a VP yet."

For decades, I encountered subtle—*and sometimes overt*—feedback rooted in other people's projections, expectations, and unresolved wounds.

I treated each moment as an initiation.

Am I intimidating? Or are *they* intimidated?

And whose responsibility is that to resolve?

For too long, healing and leadership have been treated as separate realms—one private, the other public. But the patterns we don't heal will inevitably show up in how we influence, manage, and relate to others.

Often unconsciously.

Unprocessed trauma doesn't stay locked away in our past; it shapes how we lead, relate, wield power, resolve conflict, and navigate uncertainty. Many of us unintentionally bring unexamined wounds, inherited beliefs, and reactive patterns into leadership. Whether you are leading a family, a team, or a movement, you may be doing so through the lens of your own conditioning—mistaking familiarity for fact, because it's all you've known.

We think we are making independent decisions, but in reality, many of us are just repeating patterns that have been running for generations. The key to healing and personal transformation is recognizing these cycles for what they are: conditioning. Then choosing intentionally which ones to break, which to heal, and which to pass forward.

| | Fragmented | Coherent |
|---|---|---|
| **Awareness** | Blind spots dominate; reactive to triggers; disconnected from field, self, and others. | Sees patterns clearly; attuned to body, mind, and field; able to respond with clarity. |
| **Leadership** | Defaults to force and fear; authority imposed, not earned; power over others. | Influence flows naturally; inspires trust and collaboration; power shared with others. |
| **Intentionality** | Distracted; pulled by urgency and external pressure; decisions drift from values. | Acts with clarity and purpose; aligned choices; energy directed toward vision. |
| **Growth** | Avoids discomfort; repeats old cycles; skeptical of reflection and transformation. | Embraces learning; uses friction as fuel; evolves through reflection and integration. |
| **Navigation** | Reactive to circumstances, scattered focus; movement without meaningful progress. | Guided by vision and values; adjusts course with purpose and responsiveness. |
| **Embodiment** | Says one thing, does another; conflicted energy; presence feels inconsistent. | Walks the talk; embodies alignment; presence guides others naturally. |
| **Discernment** | Clouded by ego, fear, or comparison; difficulty distinguishing truth from noise. | Anchored in inner authority; listens deeply; makes choices from clarity and integrity. |

**Fragmented vs. Quantum Leadership:** This comparison reveals how energy influences behavior. Fragmentation keeps us reactive and divided; coherence returns us to awareness, alignment, and embodied integrity. Each column and row invites reflection: are we reacting or are we responding intentionally?

Every experience, every interaction, is an opportunity to either fragment further or reclaim more of your true self.

Fragmentation lowers our frequency—scattering our energy, diluting our presence, and diminishing the impact we have. When unexamined wounds drive leadership, decision-making becomes reactive rather than intentional, leading to cultures of fear, disengagement, and burnout. Leaders operating from survival mode create environments where psychological safety is low, turnover is high, and innovation is stifled.

Whether personal or professional, individual or collective, transformation requires recognizing how past wounds influence present behavior, and then actively working to rewire these patterns. Wounds are not the only variable shaping how we lead, but they are one of the most potent. Even subtle imprints can become the hidden gears driving our default styles, until we learn to see and shift them.

**Early experiences shape the foundation of who we become in positions of power and authority. We lead as we were led, unless we *choose* to unlearn.**

As children, what we see, we internalize. We inherit not just our genetics but unconscious blueprints for leadership, power, and protection. These traits are not innate—they're survival mechanisms passed down or obtained through our own lived experiences.

If parents or other idolized figures respond to stress with anger or avoidance, we learn to do the same. If authentic expression was punished, we struggle with imposter syndrome or a fear of being seen. If emotional expression was not met with approval, vulnerability becomes uncomfortable. If expressing anger led to punishment, we learn to avoid confrontation as adults.

When our primary caregivers ignore, neglect, and de-prioritize our needs, we learn to do the same. When boundaries aren't modeled, shame, codependency, or fear of abandonment take root.

When control is modeled as power, we learn to lead through dominance.

We inherit cycles from our broader environment too: communities, cultures, social systems. Many leaders unconsciously equate control with safety—leading from perfectionism, hyper-independence, or a need to appear invincible. These are often survival patterns developed to navigate environments where vulnerability was unsafe or invalidated.

All of these patterns are born from what was modeled, spoken or unspoken. Behaviors that are rewarded get repeated. These ingrained patterns don't just shape our inner world; they inevitably spill into the way we lead. Every unresolved cycle shows up in how we set boundaries, make decisions, and handle conflict. What begins as family patterning becomes the unconscious template for leadership behavior.

As a complex-PTSD survivor, I find nervous system regulation and research on trauma particularly intriguing. Judith Herman's research suggests that long-term trauma exposure rewires self-perception, often making individuals hypervigilant, emotionally detached, or overly self-reliant—traits that may serve us in high-pressure environments but hinder emotional connection and trust-building.[15] Bessel van der Kolk found that unprocessed trauma gets stored in the body and—in an attempt to release—manifests as chronic stress, emotional suppression, and burnout, often leading to perfectionism, hyper-independence, or control-seeking behaviors in leadership.[16]

The Polyvagal Theory explains that trauma disrupts nervous system regulation, keeping us locked in fight, flight, freeze, or fawn states. This affects decision-making, adaptability, and relational capacity. Christina Maslach's research on burnout echoes this, confirming that chronic stress is often the result of toxic work cultures that prioritize profit over people.[17] Jeffrey Pfeffer expands on this by showing that work-related stress is a silent epidemic, leading to widespread health crises, disengagement, and unsustainable turnover rates.

**Unhealed fragmentation distorts leadership—turning power into performance, and presence into pressure.**

Leaders with unresolved fragmentation often overcompensate through urgency, compliance, and the pursuit of power and status. When emotional maturity and Energetic Intelligence are underdeveloped, leaders default to control or reactivity.

Living in misalignment doesn't just exhaust the body; it erodes intuition, self-trust, and fulfillment. Burnout is often a symptom of fragmentation, not just overwork. It disconnects us from the clarity required to lead from wholeness.

Without self-awareness, we risk carrying fragmented patterns into positions of power, mistaking survival instincts for effective influence and leadership. These distortions create misalignment between who we are and how we lead. Avoiding inner repair or choosing not to pursue wholeness fractures our presence, erodes coherence, and diminishes regenerative influence. In an effort to mask insecurity, leaders tend to default to patterns that resemble authoritarian or narcissistic styles that increase burnout, disconnection, and turnover.

Fragmented leaders—those who have not confronted their own trauma, biases, or fears—often lead from a place of inner turmoil. They posture, project, and protect themselves, reacting instead of responding.

Fragmentation doesn't always look like abuse of power—it can show up in more subtle, normalized patterns of overfunctioning or emotional detachment. The perfectionist who micromanages because they cannot tolerate perceived failure, especially if it might look bad on *them*. Or the charismatic but manipulative leader who uses emotional tactics to maintain control. The disconnected visionary who chases expansion at the cost of sustainability, neglecting the people and relationships that make lasting progress possible. Or the ruthless leader who prioritizes dominance over collective progress and shared well-being—all reinforcing toxic competition.

Without awareness, inherited cycles silently dictate our choices, relationships, and leadership styles. Protection rooted in fear becomes limitation. Feedback shaped by fragmentation can hold people back under the guise of helping them fit into a system that is ready to evolve.

Leaders who rise or acquire power without repairing their fragmentation are more likely to be impulsive, less empathetic, and more prone to unethical decision-making.[18] This makes them more likely to use control instead of collaboration, relying on power *over* rather than *with* and *through*.

A leader's presence starts within. Personal fragmentation shapes leadership behavior.

Fragmentation—stemming from unresolved trauma or repeated micro misalignments—creates friction and stagnant energy that prevents us from stepping fully into our truth and our power. Our greatest contribution to the collective shift—and where our control lies—is through personal transformation, organizing fragmented parts into a coherent whole and pursuing self-transcendence.

Repairing fragmentation requires confronting the unconscious patterns that shape behavior—integrating emotions and experiences and shifting from reactionary, command-and-control leadership to intentional, values-based leadership. Without repair, leadership remains reactive, fragile, and dependent on positional authority—rather than rooted in coherence, trust, and sustainable impact.

## FRAGMENTED LEADERSHIP IS THE MOST EXPENSIVE LIABILITY ON EARTH

It silently bleeds resources: trust, engagement, innovation, well-being, and long-term sustainability. The cost shows up in burnout, turnover, toxic cultures, unethical decisions, and teams that operate in survival instead of synergy. Toxic workplace cultures and poor leadership cost US companies over $223 billion in turnover alone over a five-year period.[19] But the true cost runs deeper: fractured trust, diminished creativity, and a systemic inability to lead through complexity.

Fragmentation hides in plain sight.

Overworking. Overdelivering. Overcompensating.

It looks like ambition. But beneath the surface, it's still rooted in survival. The kind that distorts truth and feigns openness while clinging tightly to power. The kind that prioritizes self-preservation and is too burned out to care. The kind that chokes a system in the name of efficiency and profit maximization.

Fragmentation shows up in the leader who says, "I'm so proud of how far you've come," while the team nods through gritted teeth, knowing they succeeded in spite of their manager—not because of them. Or the "I'll speak last" leader who postures as inclusive while never actually changing their mind.

I've sat in rooms where leaders were drowning—running on autopilot, checked out, barely surviving arbitrary deadlines, unrealistic expectations, and a calendar of bullshit meetings.[20]

And I've seen the most dangerous kind: the leader so enamored with power and control that they will uphold any system that keeps them on top. No matter the cost.

**The more fragmented the leader, the more dissonance they create—within themselves and the systems they touch.**

When our nervous systems are stuck in survival mode, the brain reorganizes around immediate self-preservation. The amygdala takes the driver's seat, scanning for threats, while the prefrontal cortex—our center for empathy, vision, and ethical decision-making—goes offline. At the same time, our reward circuitry pulls us toward immediate relief or gain, while the neural networks that regulate trust and social attunement weaken. This is why fragmentation doesn't remain an isolated, personal problem; it rewires how we engage with the world. At scale, it produces cultures defined by scarcity, individualism, and mistrust—reinforcing the very cycles of disconnection and dysfunction that stall collective progress.

**Misalignment at the top cascades into misalignment everywhere.**

When misalignment drives strategy, patterns like war, poverty, and division persist—sustained by the comfort of familiarity rather than the courage to evolve.

We currently live in a system where CEO pay continues to soar while frontline workers struggle to make rent. Where profits matter more than people, shareholder satisfaction is prioritized over planetary progress, and conscious capitalism is dismissed as idealistic because fear and domination are still the primary operating system among global leaders.

Fear of losing power. Fear of appearing weak. Fear of acknowledging harm.

Fear of what true equity might demand.

**Leadership no longer relies solely on positional authority; it is about presence, integrity, and coherence.**

Qualities that emerge only when we do the deep inner work to heal fragmentation and lead from a place of wholeness.

Restoring inner coherence is the foundation upon which transformational external leadership is built.

Coaching, therapy, and repeated reflection helped me understand that I masked my need for safety as control, perfectionism, and chasing external achievements. My hyperindependence wasn't strength—it was a protective mechanism.

When we begin to recognize and rewrite inherited scripts—when we reclaim our frequency, energetic integrity, power, programming, and Inner Authority—we can lead ourselves from wholeness instead of survival.

But healing alone isn't the end goal—especially for those called to serve.

## HEALING FRAGMENTATION *IS* THE HIDDEN LEADERSHIP ADVANTAGE

It unlocks awareness and capacity to tune in to and consciously influence energy. Neuroscience confirms that intentional repetition strengthens the prefrontal cortex—the part of our brain responsible for decision-making and impulse control—reducing amygdala reactivity, allowing leaders to respond rather than react under pressure.[21]

I've witnessed all forms of leadership—from those driven by fragmentation to extraordinary leaders whose presence was grounding—their feedback sharp but compassionate. Having done their own work, they created space for wholeness and welcomed my full presence, empowering me to expand. With them, I didn't have to brace myself before speaking. I didn't have to hide my uniqueness to feel safe.

With them, I grew.

Research continues to reinforce the same truth: organizations that prioritize well-being, psychological safety, and conscious leadership don't just succeed; they set the new standard for sustainable impact.

The future of leadership is not about extraction—it is about elevation.

Leaders who have done their own emotional work create psychologically safe workplaces, while unhealed trauma often manifests as fear-based, control-driven leadership.[22]

Leaders with regulated nervous systems create environments where people feel valued, motivated, and free to contribute without fear. When leaders cultivate self-mastery, they lead from coherence—directing their energy with clarity, integrity, and expansive authority.

When we heal, we don't just become better individuals; we become the leaders our families, our communities, and the world needs—recalibrating the energetic baseline of the systems we're part of.

Every step toward self-actualization naturally extends outward, shaping the way we engage with others, make decisions, and lead. Healing is essential—for ourselves and for the world we are actively co-creating.

**The more we regulate our own internal world, the greater stability we provide for those we lead.**

As self-leadership deepens, the impact of internal evolution ripples outward, influencing others' transformation, thus shaping leadership at every level. First, we lead ourselves through healing, self-awareness, and upgrading our encoded frequencies. Then, we influence those closest to us: our families, our inner circle, and the next generation. In the process, our influence expands outward as we heed the call to lead boldly in workplaces, communities, and beyond.

Pursuing wholeness and alignment is a personal and collective imperative.

When we heal, we don't just transform ourselves; we transform the spaces we occupy, the relationships we nurture, and the systems we influence. When we clear inner distortion, we unlock a new level of transformational precision: Energetic Intelligence or EnQ.

Energetic Intelligence is the ability to connect with and attune to the quantum field—the energy that underlies our environment—and then leverage that insight to live in alignment with your individual and collective purpose.

My life's experiences taught me that survival, resilience, and self-sacrifice were the unspoken expectations. The idea that success equaled safety was deeply ingrained, but what I failed to realize for years was that success, at least as society defines it, was not the same as healing.

I pushed forward, achieved and overperformed, believing that was the way to break cycles of struggle. But I was still carrying the weight of my wounds: hyperindependence, emotional self-sufficiency, and a deeply conditioned drive to prove my worth.

When I paused to examine these patterns, I realized changing our external circumstances starts with repairing the operating system within. The deeper I explored this work, the more clearly I saw how misalignment at the individual level shapes misalignment in the systems we lead, and the transformation that becomes possible when leaders choose coherence and conscious leadership.

To break free from these patterns, we must first recognize them. The path to wholeness isn't linear, and leadership, like healing, requires regular intentional recalibration. Consistently choosing new ways of *being*.

**Healing is not just personal—it is the first and most essential step in leadership—and it starts with ourselves.**

It's important to note that this lens of Quantum Leadership and Energetic Intelligence emerges from a predominantly Western, US-based context shaped by post-WWII individualism. While autonomy and self-determination have spurred innovation, they have also contributed to fragmentation and disconnection.

Quantum Leadership is accessible only through personal transformation, returning to ourselves with clarity to integrate fragmentation into coherent forward momentum. To be clear, this isn't a call for more individualism. Rather it's the recognition that repairing the self is the paradoxical first step to reshaping systems and relationships *beyond* ourselves.

## THE GREATEST LEADERS ARE THOSE WHO FIRST LEARN TO LEAD THEMSELVES

With expanded self-awareness and increased personal power comes responsibility to wield that influence with wisdom, integrity, and intention. Developing these skills provides you with the capacity to confidently lead with clarity, coherence, and aligned action.

Healing fragmentation is not about fixing what's broken; it's about remembering who we were before the world told us who to be. From that place of integrity, we begin to lead differently. Leaders who do this work unlock a powerful advantage: they elevate their own capacity while amplifying the potential of the people and systems they influence.

Healing fragmentation is the foundation of Quantum Leadership.

Leadership leaves a residue, an energetic imprint. Sometimes it's safety. Sometimes it's shame. It doesn't stay contained—it vibrates through people, teams, families, communities, organizations, and entire systems as accepted norms. When left unacknowledged, it becomes culture, and "the way it's always been."

**Quantum Leadership is not about control; it's about the impact of our presence.**

In my time at Amazon, I witnessed how quickly leadership style, approach, and demeanor could shift culture and shape organizational behavior.

During the pandemic, my vice president at Amazon made themselves regularly visible, inviting open dialogue and practicing appreciative inquiry. Their presence created a reinforcing loop of trust and accountability. The team responded with high standards, rapid delivery, and exceptional results under pressure. Contrast this with another vice president who was largely absent, surfacing mainly on LinkedIn or in top-down broadcasts while neglecting to model or enforce cross-functional collaboration. Their disengagement allowed silos in critical technology spaces to deepen, fueling frustration, delays, and dysfunction.

Both leaders revealed how individual alignment or misalignment—energetic frequency—propagates through culture, reinforcing either coherence or fragmentation via personal and positional authority.

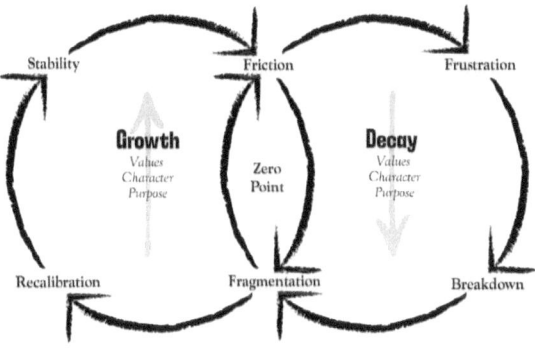

**Fuels Progress:**
- Strategic Clarity (Transparency, Purpose)
- Trust & Safety (Values, Character)
- Adaptive Coherence (Agile, Collaborative)

**Drives Dysfunction:**
- Systemic Friction (Bureaucracy, Politics)
- Misalignment (Imbalanced Decision-Making)
- Fear-Driven Culture (Blame, Deflection)

**Growth, Decay, and the Energetics of Leadership:** Misaligned leadership accelerates entropy—energy dissipates into silos, blame, and rework. Aligned leadership, on the other hand, creates entrainment—shared rhythms of trust and accountability that amplify collective performance. One loop magnifies dysfunction; the other amplifies flow.

Leaders don't just influence people. They set entire systems into motion.

Leaders sit at the center of these loops, subtly and overtly influencing probability of outcomes with the ability to interrupt dissipation and redirect energy. At the zero-point, friction becomes the choice point: energy can either spiral into flow through resonance and coherence, or collapse into entropy through frustration and fragmentation. The same loop of alignment or misalignment repeats at every layer—self, family, organization, society. A leader unconsciously dissipates energy into dysfunction, or consciously entrains coherence that cascades outward into culture, systems, and even collective consciousness.

When we think we've healed, friction shows up unexpectedly—revealing where we are still fragmented and calling us to recalibrate.

## BLINK

Seven? It's a hot, late Eastern Washington summer day, no air-conditioning in my mom's beat-up Pontiac Grand Am. I don't remember a U-Haul or packing anything in the little white house. Just all of a sudden, we're in the car and on our way to start a whole new life. Speeding west on I-90, windows down, cigarette in her hand, Alanis Morissette blaring on the stereo, the raw catharsis of *Jagged Little Pill* filling the car.

*She was happy. Like when we used to dance to Shania Twain in the living room. Those are my favorite memories of her.*

## BLINK

"We're home!" she exclaims as we pull up to a trailer park. There's fog, moisture in the air. Maybe it stopped raining recently.

Where are we?

Nothing looks familiar. Nose squished to the glass, I stare out as we drive slowly by RVs, fifth wheels, and campers. The quality slowly decreasing the longer we drive. Eventually we pull up to a dingy little one.

I feel crushed. Betrayed. Deceived.

*This is not what I had in mind when she said we were moving into a mansion.*

## BLINK

Police lights, sirens. My mom's boyfriend is driving erratically. I'm scared. My heart is pounding so hard I can hear it in my ears. Every breath feels sharp in my chest.

Why are we running from the cops?

It's dark. He's whipping down paved roads in a wooded area. Headlights flashing then vanishing as we swerve through the darkness. He quickly turns, shuts off all the lights, and speeds backward. The car jerks to a stop.

"Duck!"

The cops go right past us, one by one. The sirens fade into the distance.

# TUNING IN TO THE FIELD

> *"Behavior and development depend upon the state of the person and [their] environment...variables which are mutually dependent upon each other."*
> —KURT LEWIN

Unresolved fragmentation doesn't just live in the mind; it accumulates in the body. Time itself does nothing. Energetic blockages accumulate, layer by layer, through stress, trauma, negative thought patterns, emotional suppression, and new experiences—left unprocessed, they burrow deeper. Unresolved fragmentation leads to internal conflict and external friction, the felt tension that arises when our inner coherence clashes with our outer choices.

At some point, survival mode stops working. The effort, the overthinking, the need to control—all of it just stops being enough. The pain doesn't go away. The questions don't disappear. The physical exhaustion simply becomes unbearable.

For years, I tried to outthink my trauma. I believed that if I could just reframe my experiences, understand my patterns, and develop better coping strategies, I would feel better. I powered through life: single mother, working and going to school full-time, building a career, chasing external validation. I reached what I thought was my version of success, what society defines as success. Stability. Achievement. A life that, on the surface, looked like I had broken the cycle.

But no matter how much work I did cognitively, my body kept reacting as if I were still in danger. I hadn't *healed*—I suppressed. I played strong, wore resilience like armor, detached from my true self to fit into the mold of what I thought was required to survive and succeed.

On the surface, it looked like I was leveraging opportunity, but on the inside, an unforgiving whisper kept me constantly on edge. *Stay alert. Stay small. Don't get stuck. Don't give them more than they deserve.* But I always did. I gave too much. Stayed too long. Held on just long enough to betray myself. Fragmentation can look like commitment to deeply held beliefs, goals, and visions, but it's really just fear. Fear of letting go, of starting over, of facing the truth that *this, whatever you've been chasing*, was never going to fill the void you've been trying to run from.

---

**WHEN WE LEARN TO INTERPRET FRICTION AS DATA—TUNING IN BECOMES ONE OF OUR MOST RELIABLE GUIDES FOR PERSONAL TRANSFORMATION AND QUANTUM LEADERSHIP.**

---

Friction is how the field speaks when we're out of alignment. It is felt tension—the dissonance between our current reality and the reality the field is asking us to align with. It's a feedback loop, revealing exactly where our internal operating system needs recalibration. The more we ignore it, the louder it gets. It manifests as friction and misalignment—a signal from the field that something is ready to be seen, healed, or evolved. It is a signal and an *opportunity*—asking us to examine the choices we make and the experiences shaping them—if we're willing to listen.

Think of the body as one big antenna. The heart, the brain, and even our fascia—the connective tissue running through our body—are constantly picking up signals from the field. In early 2016 the friction I'd been ignoring became undeniable—pain demands to be felt, except I didn't know how. By 2017 my life began to unravel.

Accumulated stagnant energy stemming from a lifetime living in survival mode roared into my consciousness, demanding to be confronted and healed. Each loop, hesitation, and surge of tension I experienced was the field signaling that something needed to shift if I wanted to evolve into my purpose and do more than just survive—pointing me beyond who I thought I had to be, toward the truth of who I really am.

---

**WHEN WE'RE MISALIGNED, THE SIGNAL IS DISTORTED; WHEN WE'RE COHERENT, THE SIGNAL IS CLEAR.**

---

I spent years relying on logic, structure, and sheer willpower to move through life, to achieve, to overcome. But something deeper was pulling at me. A whisper, an instinct, a knowing I couldn't yet name—a deeper intelligence guiding me to notice stuck energy that no longer aligned with who I was becoming. The hum of static under my skin, the tightness fading from my chest, the immediate clarity when something in my life no longer fit. It was as if the air itself dissolved density. I could *feel* the pull, nudging me to release the grip and flow *with* the guidance.

Quantum physics reveals at the deepest level, we are all connected—energetically, biologically, and scientifically. The body—when we're willing to tune in—is often the first place the field whispers. If we learn to tune in early, to notice the signals in our bodies and our energy, we can respond with greater intention and more precise impact.

When we push emotions down, they manifest elsewhere: in our bodies, our relationships, and our leadership styles—restricting vitality, leaving us feeling stuck, fatigued, or disconnected, like drudging through wet cement. This energy doesn't vanish; it manifests as projection, self-sabotage, and reactive decision-making.

I resorted to the familiarity of masking my reality because the environment demanded it, once again. That's what strong people do, right?

They rise above. They don't complain. They don't dwell in the pain.

They power through.

That's not strength. That's suppression.

It blocks emotions, energy, and growth. It manifests as stress, anxiety, and autoimmune disorders.[23] It sneaks into your nervous system, tightening your chest, shortening your breath, making your body a battleground for all the emotions you refuse to acknowledge.

## FRICTION IS FEEDBACK—THE FIELD'S WAY OF INVITING US TO SLOW DOWN, REASSESS, AND REALIGN

From 2017 to 2023, I worked through the realization that everything that had once been my greatest strength—my independence, my drive, my ability to cut through bullshit and get things done—was suddenly the very thing holding me back from evolving into the person I really wanted to be.

That awareness could have turned into shame. But instead, it became an opening.

*Would I let the external world determine the next version of me or would I rise from within?*

For years, I was running full tilt—leading large teams, delivering results, and keeping my personal world carefully walled off from my professional one. On the surface, I was achievement-driven, organized, and in control. But beneath that, a constant friction point existed: the gap between who I was, who I wanted to become, and who the environment demanded. I learned to perform at the edge of that tension, holding my ground where I could and bending where I felt I had to.

Energy surged and swirled through me with a ferocity I'd never felt before; at times it shimmered like glitter in my veins, spilling slowly into the air around me, and at others it sliced through me like jagged shards of ice, stabbing every cell. Sensational experiences came in waves: sudden vertigo, drifting detachment, floods of memory, overwhelming emotional release. The shifts were undeniable—the evidence showed up in my nerves, my breath, my skin.

The subtle signals, friction we keep powering through, is one of our best access points to begin understanding felt frequency and Energetic Intelligence. Friction invites us into inquiry, and inquiry anchors us in the body—where alignment can be felt. Our body is our tuning fork; it translates our intuition into action, words, and something that the five senses, our physical world, can comprehend and make sense of.

Later, I'd come to recognize this as the foundation for Energetic Intelligence (EnQ): the capacity to interpret internal and external signals, and to lead ourselves toward coherence rather than collapse. Energetic Intelligence becomes the data set by which you process the feedback between your internal coherence and external experience.

Tuning in to the field is how we learn to listen.

Tuning in is noticing what pulls us closer to harmony and what signals contraction or internal static. Tuning in to friction energetically turns distortion into data and friction into a powerful opportunity for realignment.

Healing is what determines whether we lead from coherence or control. This doesn't mean we'll never feel angry or upset; it's about responding differently when we do.

We live in a world that rewards fake happiness, false bravado. The pressure to be happy all the time. Cultural conditioning teaches us to bypass or label friction as negativity—we avoid discomfort, pretend everything is fine, and expect others to do the same.

But repair and transformation require sitting with discomfort, not glossing over it.

Resilience is more than enduring struggle. It's learning to navigate it with self-awareness, self-compassion, and intentional response. Friction itself is not the enemy. True power and strength is having the ability to acknowledge and move through reality without letting it consume you. When we label discomfort as negativity and dismiss it, we bypass the very signals meant to bring us back into alignment.

Living in alignment and leading from coherence starts with tuning in—creating the space to notice, feel, and choose between stimulus and response. When we are calm and regulated, we make aligned choices. But when we are stressed, dysregulated, or reactive—we fuel chaos and dysfunction.

The ability to consciously respond to friction is what allows us to release old energy and take steps that close the tragic gap between who we are right now and who we truly want to be.

## IT'S UP TO US TO TUNE IN, BUT THE SIGNS ARE ALWAYS THERE

Every moment of friction is a moment to pause and reflect. *Am I going to continue repeating the familiar, or am I ready to step into something new?*

What we suppress emotionally, we carry physically; when we think we're stuck we're actually feeling the friction of inherited coding and unhealed fragmentation. While we often use words like "stuck" or "resistance" interchangeably, friction is slightly different. Friction is the immediate felt tension that invites us to realign before patterns of conflict crystallize into deeper burnout or total collapse.

Consciously or subconsciously telling ourselves we must *stay positive* at all costs often does more harm than good. It suppresses real emotions, discourages self-reflection, and forces people into emotional bypassing rather than addressing underlying dynamics. The goal is not to eliminate struggle but to develop the tools to move through it with grace.

Genuine optimism is grounded in realism; it helps us acknowledge pain and uncertainty while still choosing hope and aligned action. It allows space for challenges and the flexibility to view life through multiple lenses rather than forcing unchecked idealism. It makes space for truth, while still choosing possibility. Recognizing the difference is essential because while bypassing can lead to denial and deeper suffering when reality doesn't match expectations, genuine optimism fosters adaptability and agility.

Friction shows up in your body first, before it ever affects behavior or our interactions with others. What you feel inside becomes the raw material for how you engage externally. My body held the pain I wasn't ready to face until it escalated into something I couldn't ignore—leading to a partial hysterectomy at twenty-nine. Trauma doesn't release through logic. It releases when we let it exist without judgment, when we allow ourselves to *feel* it. Until then, I had spent most of my life avoiding that part.

Feeling is not the enemy. You cannot heal what you refuse to feel. Sadness, anger, grief, uncertainty, resentment, shame, apathy. Emotions are not obstacles. They carry energetic signals, and open the doorway to repair.

> **FRICTION IS AN ENERGETIC GIFT. IT CARRIES INFORMATION—RESONANCE, CLARITY, DISTORTION, CONTRACTION—THAT HELPS US UNDERSTAND WHERE WE ARE ON THE SPECTRUM OF ALIGNMENT.**

We don't always get to choose the source or timing, but we get to choose what we do with the information and how we respond. When we label discomfort as negativity and dismiss it, we miss the sacred invitation to grow.

Suppression fractures inner coherence, creating fragmentation. That fragmentation generates friction—feedback from the field that signals it's time to tune in, realign, and recalibrate.

Ignoring emotions doesn't make them disappear; it just stores the energy for later. Eventually they surface as unjustified, exaggerated anger, a sudden breakdown, or chronic stress and illness. A neglected, exhausted, or overstimulated body cannot sustain the energy required for transformation. When we ignore our physical needs—rest, nourishment, movement, and stillness—we lower our capacity to process energy and emotion, making expansion harder to hold.

Every unresolved wound follows this same arc until we choose to interrupt it. The way we interpret and respond to signals leads us further into fragmentation, or closer to living in alignment. Repairing fragmentation is recognizing how our lived experiences and realities create unprocessed pain, energetic stagnation, and cycles of dysfunction. Sometimes we stall because we're being asked to pause, reflect, and integrate before making our next move. Seeing the pattern visually can help you recognize it in your own life.

**Quantum Leadership invites us to work with the field to determine where *we* need to grow to bring about desired change in ourselves and the environment.**

**Maintains Alignment:**
- Integration (Inner Authority)
- Emotional Processing (Recalibration)
- Authentic Expression (Aligned Action)

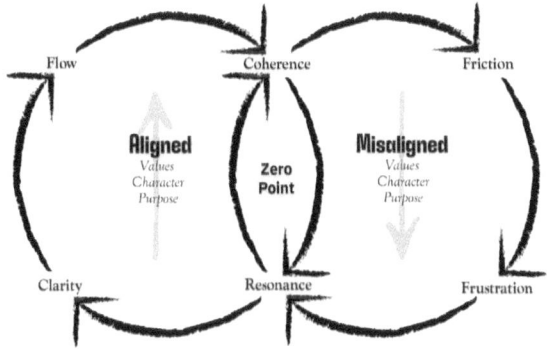

**Drives Misalignment:**
- Conditioning (Encoded Frequencies)
- Suppression & Distortion (Fragmentation)
- Overload & Overstimulation (Burnout)

**Alignment, Misalignment, and Energetic Feedback Loops:** Alignment generates flow, coherence, and resonance through integration and intentional action. Misalignment, by contrast, amplifies friction, frustration, and burnout when emotional or energetic signals are suppressed.

## FRICTION WILL SHOW YOU WHERE YOU'RE OUT OF ALIGNMENT WITH YOUR PURPOSE—*AND* WHAT'S TRYING TO EVOLVE THROUGH YOU

Evidence suggests self-directed neuroplasticity—intentional thought changes, mindfulness, and habit formation—can rewire brain circuits. The more we practice new thought patterns, the stronger those neural pathways become.[24] Rick Hanson's research on neuroplasticity confirms that the brain can restructure itself at any age when exposed to focused mental effort, visualization, and consistent behavior shifts. His work supports the idea that breaking old patterns isn't about willpower; it's about cultivating new responses and strengthening beneficial pathways.

This reinforces what I finally began to understand: healing wasn't just about reliving and releasing emotions; it was about training my *brain and body* to experience safety at the same time.

The body's integrated network—our brain, nervous system, fascia, and subtle energetic pathways—works in unity to sense, interpret, and respond to the world. It is your tool to tune in to the quantum field. It is how you move through fragmentation with awareness, and how you apply new insights to current conditions.

Once you stop performing for the world, you're left with what's underneath. That's where the real work begins, and where most people turn back, quit, or self-sabotage. You reach the edge of expansion and don't realize that what's coming next isn't collapse. It's confrontation—with yourself—with the unconscious patterns and beliefs still quietly shaping how you lead, love, and show up.

Avoidance may seem easier in the moment. Busying yourself in back-to-back meetings, overcommitting to projects, or numbing with distractions and substances, pretending everything is fine so no one notices the inner chaos.

When I finally stopped powering through, I realized I wasn't thriving. I was surviving in disguise—navigating a system that prioritized relentless execution over humanity. I tried to force myself to keep pushing, but years of unprocessed trauma and stress had already taken its toll. The goal is not to be positive all the time. It's to be authentic, aware, and intentional. Strength is allowing yourself to *feel* life.

The goal isn't to stop the waves; it's to learn how to ride them. To become so still in the current that you can clearly recognize friction for your growth. Choosing expansion allows us to break the cycles that keep us repeating the same patterns in our careers, relationships, and leadership.

The key to personal transformation is layering small actions into your existing life, turning them into automatic, effortless habits.

Healing required me to reintegrate and recalibrate every part of myself. It required returning to my trauma through a new lens, at every opportunity possible. A new level of radical responsibility, self-awareness, emotional processing, and nervous system regulation with each experience.

Healing is more than just understanding your past. It's about actively reshaping the way your brain responds to future stress, challenges, and emotional triggers. The brain is constantly firing, wiring, and rewiring, building new synapses and new neural connections through repetition, attention, and experience.

Beneath the accolades was a nervous system trained to survive, a body begging me to listen, and a leadership identity built on proving my worth to everyone but myself. Therapy helped me make sense of my story—to put words to what happened, say things out loud in a safe space. It allowed me to understand the patterns that shaped me, why I responded to certain activations, returned to similar experiences repeatedly, struggled with specific fears, and why my nervous system had been locked in survival mode for so long.

But *understanding* is not the same as *healing*.

Insights alone weren't enough. I wasn't *feeling* that energy and allowing it to move through my body. Meditation deepened my mental fitness and self-awareness, but I couldn't bypass the need for grounding and structure. Early 2021 marked the final unraveling of everything. I received my case file from the state and held on to it for six months before opening it, avoiding the truth while trying to hold my life together at work.

For years, I could recite my trauma without actually feeling it. I could explain what happened, how it impacted me, but my body still held on to the weight of it. I could talk about my experiences without releasing the emotional charge attached to them.

While trying to repair my own fragmentation, I was still chasing another promotion at Amazon, still trying to prove my worth, still maintaining the high-achieving persona that protected me for years. Behind closed doors, I was coming undone. I didn't realize it at the time, but my body was carrying years of unresolved pain—straining under every unprocessed memory and unspoken truth. The stress, the tension, the exhaustion became unbearable until there was no choice but to listen.

I carried anger I didn't allow myself to feel, grief I refused to acknowledge. I told myself I had moved on when really, I just pushed everything down deeper. When I finally gave myself permission, my fear turned into rage.

I didn't know what to do with it. So, between roles—sorting through the mess of state files and before returning to lead one of the largest cultural transformation efforts I had ever undertaken—I signed up for a half-marathon. I didn't train. I just needed to move the energy, to sweat out the static, find a way to let my body scream the things my voice hadn't yet said.

*I needed to burn off the shame that wasn't mine to absorb in the first place.*

On race day, I woke up to pouring rain and briefly contemplated not doing it—but the need to process this energy was too strong. I stepped out onto the driveway and took off running.

Lap after lap. Breath after breath. I met every memory, pain, and surge of anger head-on. Around mile ten, I broke. The only energy source I could pull from was the grit that courses through my veins. Every step, every exhale:

*Fuck you. Fuck you. Fuck you.*

I let the rage move through me. I finally stopped pretending I wasn't angry, hurt, sad, disappointed.

I was finally done running from everything my body had been carrying—energetic residue my mind refused to process: shame, rage, the accumulating cost of silencing myself—then and now.

Understanding where my pain came from was one thing. Allowing myself to feel it was another.

Friction speaks the sacred language of alignment.

Friction isn't asking you to push harder; it's asking you to pay attention.

You've likely overlooked or disregarded these signals before—

burnout, resentment, the pit in your stomach before a meeting, the "yes" you say with a clenched jaw, the quiet dread, or the decision fatigue that stalls teams in endless meetings.

In quantum terms, collapse isn't failure—it's feedback. The old system destabilizes so a new pattern can form. Things fall apart so they can be rebuilt in alignment with something greater. Destruction is not the end; it is the beginning. The old must collapse to make space for the new.

## COHERENCE GIVES US THE COURAGE AND CLARITY TO STOP REACHING OUTWARD AND BEGIN LISTENING INWARD

Healing fragmentation and restoring wholeness in pursuit of alignment is energetic recalibration. Learning to tune in to the quantum field allowed me to energetically connect with fragmented parts through my present experiences and use the present moment to heal the past.

After nearly four years of therapy and deep self-guided inner work, I came across a procedure called a *stellate ganglion block* (SGB), a treatment that can reset the body's physiological response to trauma. One day, after my third or fourth treatment, I heard the familiar, critical part of me speak up—the same one that had always been negative and filled with fear. But then another part—calm, grounded, and firm—responded:

*No, we're not doing that today.*

In that instant, the weight lifted. For the first time in my life, I had control over my own mind. A peace washed over me that I had never known before. I understood what it meant to feel nurtured—to feel a mother's love. My wholeness, my completeness, my *innate* worth suddenly felt inarguable.

Imagine a highway—the surface cracks, small indicators of deeper instability. At first, the repairs seem simple: fill the cracks, smooth the surface, make it functional again. But if you really want to create something stable, you have to tear up the foundation, dig through layers of old concrete, broken asphalt, and buried erosion. When we tune in, we dig, uncover, and dust off the pieces of ourselves that have been hidden under years of conditioning, pain, and survival.

Years of therapy helped me build new pathways—slowly rewiring the circuits in my brain and body—but survival-based defaults held strong. It was like paving beautiful roads that remained closed, visible from a distance. After a few SGB sessions, those roads finally opened. The detours, the traffic, the construction all cleared—revealing instant access to coherence. My nervous system exhaled for the first time in decades. The constant tension in my body dissolved. My mind quieted. The thoughts that used to spiral into rumination simply *stopped*.

I didn't have to *try*. I didn't have to spend precious energy fighting that critic for hours or days.

Healing isn't linear—it's cyclical, unpredictable, and often messy. It doesn't unfold in perfect stages or neat chapters, and growth rarely looks like steady progress. But when we are conscious, open, and self-aware, friction becomes a signal. It becomes a data point to remaining residue—unprocessed fragmentation and limiting beliefs—that must be addressed in order to expand or become an energetic match to that which we're attempting to align with, co-create, or call in.

Catching distortion in real time requires recognizing the internal jolt, then pausing long enough to choose your response. Transformation and recalibration starts with new awareness—intentionally navigating the friction between perception, reality, and Inner Authority to sharpen your mission, vision, and character as the old structures fall away.

It is choosing alignment, again and again, until it becomes your natural state. It is a daily practice—an intentional decision to honor yourself enough to stay coherent, grounded, and true to your values. Sustained by self-love and self-trust, alignment becomes the foundation for energetic recalibration, deeper self-awareness, and lasting transformation.

**Alignment—coherence in motion—isn't the goal. It's the ground you stand on.**

In a leadership meeting, I paused before responding when my director interjected, "Oh, I thought you were going to come out"—making a sharp, unnecessary comment about my sexuality. I was especially shocked, as this was someone who, in theory, should know better than to blurt out something like this in a professional setting.

I felt the heat rising; my mind flashed through ways to quip back. Instead, I took a deep breath, looked around the room, and smiled before picking up exactly where I'd intended. I stayed focused and made my point without handing her the reaction she may have been hoping for. What she didn't like—aside from my refusal to let all blame for organizational dysfunction fall elsewhere—was that I'm deeply comfortable in my own skin. Someone else's discomfort doesn't diminish your sense of self. Authority doesn't require conformity.

I learned that my depth—the very energy that could feel confrontational to others—was also my compass. Those attuned to it were drawn in; those resisting it often resisted *me*. Tuning in to that friction and decoding its source became my advantage, allowing me to stand in full alignment even in the most challenging moments of my career.

**Friction creates the pressure needed to move you toward actions that repattern your reality from the inside out.**

If we are unable or unwilling to heed the signals—we resist change—we cling to what no longer serves us, remain stuck in disconnection, in survival mode, reacting rather than creating. If we embrace falling apart and recognize it as an invitation to rebuild, we can consciously shape our inner world, which affects the external world, especially our sphere of influence. When you believe in yourself, you stop waiting for permission to become who you were meant to be and you begin living in coherence with who you truly are. You begin living from your Inner Authority, in coherence with your aligned self.

| | Definition | Why It Matters |
|---|---|---|
| **Resonance** | When things click and feel in sync. | Builds trust and amplifies presence. |
| **Coherence** | Mind, body, and actions are aligned. | Foundation of clarity and impact. |
| **Attunement** | Sensing subtle signals. | Helps spot misalignment early. |
| **Energetic Intelligence** | Using energy patterns wisely. | Turns presence into influence. |
| **Misalignment** | Internal conflict or contradiction. | Dilutes trust and effectiveness. |

**Energetic Definitions:** Core terminology within Quantum Leadership and their relevance to overall effectiveness.

Coherence is energetic clarity—knowing who you are, what you value, and what you're here to do, even when external conditions try to shake your certainty. Conviction—in yourself, your purpose, or something greater—is fundamental to Inner Authority and Quantum Leadership. Your growth, development, and the shedding of old layers are all part of the process of self-actualization and transcendence. When we reclaim our whole selves, we regain the ability to discern between distortion and developmentally accurate signals.

Being "stuck" is an invitation to slow down, to recognize the patterns you've outgrown, and to shift from survival-based success to soul-aligned leadership. Once we learn to recognize the static of fragmentation, we can begin to tune in to the signal of alignment.

When we learn to listen we don't just avoid burnout—we evolve—we transform from the inside out. The question isn't whether we'll face friction. It's whether we'll use it as pressure to perform or as permission to transform and expand.

Life and leadership are no longer about power and force.

They're about tuning in to flow, and trusting what you sense to be necessary for your growth in *that moment*.

When we're fragmented we don't hear frequency—we hear fear.

When you practice being fully present, you reduce suffering.

Emotions become temporary experiences rather than overpowering forces.

**Friction—emotional, relational, or energetic—is not a flaw. It is a special feature, the operating signal that prompts recalibration toward alignment.**

Every friction point is simply an invitation to come home to yourself—in service of your role within the current collective mission and the greater work of transformation.

Fragmentation is the root cause, friction is the signal, and tuning in is the path to recalibration, Energetic Intelligence, and Quantum Leadership. Tuning in allows us to loosen our grip—on control, outcome, identity—and begin trusting the deeper current of our Inner Authority, our calling, our unfolding purpose.

As we align within, the signal we emit shifts, subtly influencing the field around us. Inner alignment doesn't *cause* the field to change on its own, but it increases the probability of systemic coherence by shifting how we engage with and influence our environment.

Every moment carries a frequency and infinite possible outcomes. Tuning in to the field asks us to go beyond, *what am I feeling?* And asks us to inquire instead, *what am I tuned in to, what is it telling me about my growing edge, and how is it shaping the way I show up for others?*

Living in alignment means recognizing the moments when friction reveals fragmentation—and using that signal to return to coherence the moment you become aware. By tuning in to bodily and quantum signals, we create the foundation for lasting transformation.

## BLINK

Back to the trailer.

*I hated that trailer. I'm convinced it's the source of my claustrophobia.*

I watch my mom get physically abused. My brother and I are repeatedly exposed to sexually explicit material and live sex. It's not the first time.

## BLINK

Screaming. Yelling. The camper shaking. My brother and I huddle in the corner. Glass shatters. The next thing I know, we're in the car, driving aimlessly, looking for a hospital—and my mom isn't using one of her arms.

*Years later, while driving to work, I rounded a bend I'd taken countless times before. Out of nowhere—boom—I was back there. And then, just as suddenly, I was walking into work to run an operation, focusing on metrics and decisions that felt so small in the grand scheme of things.*

## BLINK

Eight? We move a lot from trailer park to trailer park. My mom is regularly physically abused, and she's become mean and abusive too.

I don't like her anymore. I don't like her boyfriend either.

They are in full-blown meth addiction. We never have money for anything. My little brother and I eat crumbs out of old cereal bags or dry Top Ramen.

One day, we come back and our trailer is gone.

We're homeless.

*Probably because they preferred to get high and didn't pay our site fee. No warning, no time to gather what little we had. We slept in the Pathfinder that night.*

*At least we had a roof—of sorts.*

## BLINK

Eight? Nine? We move into a one-bedroom apartment in Bremerton, just off of a busy street and then down several outdoor flights of stairs to a landing zone. A walking path leads to our front door. The adults use the living room as their bedroom. When they want to get high, they make my brother and me stay in our room.

I missed half a year of second grade, and worry about whether or not I'll be able to move on to third grade when we go to enroll in school.

*Why are they so bad at taking care of us?*

I learn that survival is a skill. Feeding yourself, cleaning clothes, navigating the world alone—these things aren't hard. I learn how to do laundry. I carry my hamper up the two or three flights of stairs to the laundromat. Detergent on top of the dirty clothes, quarters in my pocket.

*Taking care of myself was not hard. But understanding why the people meant to protect me couldn't even protect themselves—that was impossible to understand.*

## BLINK

I'm in third grade in Bremerton. I open our fridge and find nothing but broken eggshells. I don't know why anyone would put broken eggs back in the fridge, but there are no eggs left, just empty eggshells. There is nothing else in the fridge. My mom and stepdad are asleep in the middle of the day.

I can't wait for school. To get away from them.

To eat.

## BLINK

At one point things get better. It doesn't stay like that for very long. It never does.

A regular day, interrupted by three loud knocks on the door: "Police, open up! Police, open up."

My stepdad says not to open the door, then sends us to our room. My brother and I listen as the police break down the door, barrel in, and arrest our parents. I don't know what they're looking for, but they destroy every part of the apartment. They take everything out of every single drawer, even mine and my brother's.

*I didn't realize until my mid-thirties that this memory was connected to another memory I'd carried separately my whole life.*

*That happens a lot.*

Not long after, I'm living with my mom's friend and spending most days with her daughter and her daughter's friends—teenagers twice my age—jumping fences and sneaking into pool parties.

*At the time, it felt like freedom. Only later did I understand I was probably there to stay out of foster care. I still don't know how long I stayed with them, or where my brother or mom were.*

### BLINK

We're at Goodwill. My mom's frantically searching. "We all need nice clothes for court!" She's tweaking, but has enough wherewithal to execute manipulation. She's hoping that parading "family" in front of the court will help obtain a lighter sentence for her husband.

It works.

# INTENTION

>>>>>>>>

DEFINE GOALS AND STRATEGIC DIRECTION; ASSESS AGAINST STATED VALUES

# RECALIBRATING THE FIELD

*"We see, we feel, we change."*
—JOHN P. KOTTER

In a world that rewards false positivity and relentless performance, we often dismiss the very signals guiding our transformation. We're taught to perform at the expense of acknowledging friction. Leaders avoid hard conversations, allowing toxic behavior to persist. Organizations cling to outdated processes despite declining results.

What exists inside inevitably shapes what emerges in our lives. When we leave fragmentation unexamined, it ripples through the organizations and communities we are a part of, manifesting as unethical leadership, leadership breakdowns, and systemic dysfunction.

Friction arises not only in our body and mind but also in the field around us—the environments, systems, and relationships we move through. Our interaction with others reveals where we are aligned, and where unhealed fractures still drive our leadership. How we respond in those moments either strengthens trust and growth or accelerates breakdown and stagnation.

After escaping an abusive relationship, working a full-time job while finishing my undergrad degree, and then securing a life-changing opportunity at a prestigious company like Amazon, I believed I had broken the cycle.

I told myself I was fine because I "made it."

But *making it* and living in alignment are not the same.

Patterns began to emerge—familiar loops I was unconsciously repeating. In these moments, friction exposes whether we're leading from alignment or avoiding the deeper work—inviting us to listen more deeply, recalibrate, and show up differently.

Tuning in to your frequency during friction or conflict with others means sensing how the interaction is affecting your state and consciously choosing to recalibrate before responding—influencing culture, decisions, and the environments we create together. Otherwise the same patterns, triggers, and emotional reactions repeat themselves; you begin to believe, *this is just who I am*.

When we ignore friction—the energetic signals inviting us into deeper alignment—we're prone to swing between one of two extremes: victimhood, where we stay stuck in disempowerment and external blame, or toxic positivity, where we mask discomfort with false bravado and bypass the real work. We're taught that staying positive is strength, but more often it's suppression—bypassing discomfort and dismissing pain in the name of resilience.

## FRICTION REVEALS DISSONANCE—THE SPACE BETWEEN WHO YOU *TRULY* ARE AND HOW YOU'VE BEEN OPERATING

From 2017 to 2023, most of my energy was consumed by healing—working through complex-PTSD, rebuilding my identity, and reclaiming my purpose. As I deepened that work, I began noticing how my presence shifted when I was grounded in my values versus when I was operating from habit or expectation. Colleagues responded differently when I led from alignment—trust deepened, conversations opened, and collaboration felt natural. But when I was disconnected from my core, I defaulted to overachievement and control, pushing harder.

The shifts we make within ourselves inevitably repattern the environments we influence, like two sides of a Möbius strip. What begins in private shows up in how we lead, shape systems, and impact collective outcomes.

Healing wasn't something I did after work. It *was* the work. I learned to recalibrate myself, but the real test began with how that conviction collided and harmonized with the world around me.

As my own alignment deepened, what once felt tolerable became intolerable. The more I reclaimed my Inner Authority, the less willing I was to resonate with environments built on dysfunction. Unclear communication, blurred roles, and cultures resistant to shared learning fracture shared vision and capacity. Leaders may appear effective, while quietly eroding trust with endless meetings, unnecessary bureaucracy, and poor organizational health.

**What we haven't confronted within ourselves will always find a way to manifest externally.**

Friction isn't only an individual experience; it emerges in the spaces between us when our unresolved patterns meet the fragmentation of others. Left unacknowledged, this clash can spiral chaotically, fueled by ego and societal conditioning. But when noticed and held with intention, the same friction becomes a doorway into intentional growth and expansion—revealing our blueprint and giving us the chance to choose coherence instead of collapse.

Energetic recalibration is the intentional act of using the

present moment to restore personal coherence—shifting patterns, triggers, and emotional reactions so they no longer run on autopilot.

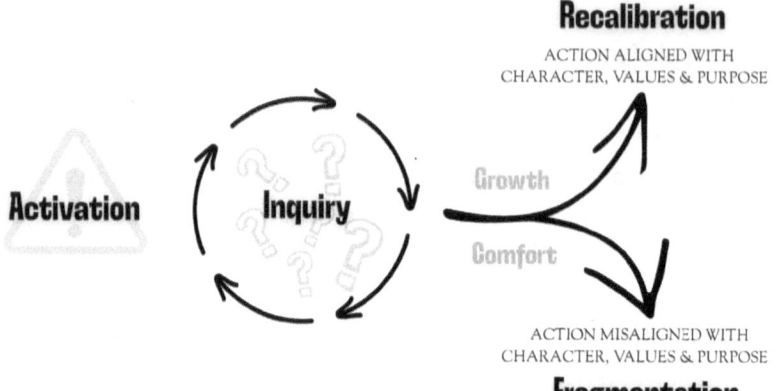

**Energetic Recalibration:** Recalibration begins when we pause long enough to sense what's happening beneath the surface. This illustrates how awareness interrupts automatic reactions, creating the space to realign intention and behavior. Transformation isn't forceful; it's responsive, guided by presence and energetic integrity.

Our bodies are not separate from our consciousness. They are the physical expression of our soul, the vessel through which we experience, expand, and *feel* energy. Neuroscience and physiology show that our emotions and intentions create patterns in the energetic field, influencing not only our personal well-being but the energy or frequency we emit.

When power is involved, the impact intensifies—inequities widen, unspoken dynamics reverberate further, and the impact of our personal tragic gap becomes impossible to ignore.

What I had once intellectualized as dissonance or incoherence (burnout or anxiety) now pulsed through my body as either contraction or clarity. When friction arises—especially in relationships, teams, or cultures—we can use it as a prompt to either expand into wholeness, or retreat into protection. When we avoid this work, our communication with the field becomes clouded, and we misinterpret signals through the lens of old wounds. To receive undistorted signals, we repair our fragmentation via integration, or energetic recalibration.

---

> **OUR INNER GUIDANCE SYSTEM EMITS AND SENSES ENERGETIC FREQUENCY. THE ENERGY YOU BRING INTO A ROOM—THE FRICTION, THE FLOW, THE FRAGMENTATION, OR THE COHERENCE—MATTERS MORE THAN ANYTHING YOU SAY.**

---

Unhealed trauma distorts our energetic frequency, making it harder to accurately read others and the systems around us. When we heal, recalibrate, and regulate, our body becomes a more accurate receiver—able to sense what's true and aligned in real time. Until then, distortion shapes how we respond to authority, use positional power, and interpret feedback from the field.

## ENERGETIC ATTUNEMENT AND RECALIBRATION ISN'T A BYPASS—IT'S A BRIDGE

Recalibrating the mind and the body is healing—tuning in is about how our nervous system responds to the world. Emotional and energetic regulation occurs through the brain-body connection but is ultimately ruled by the nervous system. Tuning in to your frequency during friction or conflict with others is an act of energetic recalibration.

This act of tuning in—especially in the presence of others—moves beyond belief or dogma into inner knowing. When practiced intentionally, it becomes the entry point to Energetic Intelligence (EnQ).

Energetic recalibration begins the moment you pause to sense the dynamics beneath the surface—subtle shifts in your body, emotions, and environment—and consciously adjust your inner state until mind, body, and energy return to coherence. It's this recalibration that transforms awareness into aligned action.

Unresolved fragmentation or energetic residue from past experiences accumulates. Layer upon layer of unprocessed strain builds pressure in the system until burnout isn't just about overwork but about the accumulated weight of everything left unhealed.

For some, the journey to coherence is a slow unfolding. For others, it erupts with a disruptive force—so profound that it dismantles everything they thought they knew.

For a year and a half, I lived in the abyss. I experienced hardship before, but not like this. Nothing that reached so deeply into my core, unraveling every illusion, burning away every false identity I built for protection. It was relentless, a slow and painful shedding of everything I thought I knew about myself.

It felt like my soul had stepped outside of my body, like I was moving through life but not entirely in it. Ego death, often described as an enlightening experience, can also feel like chaos and destruction when not properly understood or navigated in safety. Some nights, I sat in the dark, rocking back and forth, trying to breathe through the intensity of it. Other nights, I sobbed uncontrollably, no desire to keep going—not that I wanted to literally die, but I wanted the pain to. I was exhausted, tired of fighting my own mind. Tired of the inner critic, the memories, the endless unraveling.

For some, ego death is the realization that the self is an artificial construct, shaped by societal conditioning.[25] I think it's also the collapse that precedes the zero point, where identity and old structures dissolve and the field of possibility begins to open.

This was my initiation. The breaking point before the breakthrough. The moment when resonance with the field was no longer just a concept but an absolute necessity for survival.

I wanted peace. But peace felt impossible when I was drowning in my own fragmented remnants. As painful as it was, I came to learn that the pain isn't there to break you; it's there to purge you—to strip away everything that isn't truly *you*.

I found myself zoning out in meetings and struggling to remember conversations. My mind was a constant battleground. I didn't realize it then, but this was my body's final warning. It was as if my soul had stopped participating in life, leaving my physical vessel to deal with the fallout. Regardless of the root case, burnout is a prime example of what happens when we ignore friction's early whispers.

For years, I'd show up to work exhausted after having been up all night battling flashbacks or chronic pain. Exclusion or moments of friction often sent me spiraling into imposter syndrome. I'd overcompensate to prove myself, only to realize later that the distortion wasn't mine—it was in the system. Each cycle forced me to recalibrate, stand for ethical use of power, and face the relational fallout that often follows resonance rejection—when coherence amplifies dissonance in the environment because your presence exposes the unresolved distortions and insecurities of the system or those with greater positional authority.

**You can't control the field, but you can become coherent enough to move with it.**

Healing and transformation isn't just about making sense of your past; it's about figuring out what tools and systems work specifically for you to achieve and *maintain* coherence. It's learning to retrain and manage your operating system, shift emotional patterns, and increase self-awareness. It's about exploring in safety and developing new (more intentional) responses to triggers or activations.

Tuning in to your frequency—or the field—means sensing your body's signals and regulating them, shifting from automatic reactions to intentional responses, and creating space for deliberate choice. It's the practice of attuning without absorbing, discerning meaning, and preparing for recalibration. It's the signal to the quantum field that you're ready to meet the moment, moving from the messy middle into alignment with the field, where your choices shape what emerges.

While in college, my former employer and I discussed a specific salary increase post-graduation. When tone and enthusiasm shifted in follow-up conversations, Energetic Intelligence began signaling a different, more aligned path forward.

Shortly after that, I came across a website about Amazon recruiting recent college graduates. Before then, Amazon wasn't even on my radar. I thought I wanted the path I could see in front of me—until suddenly another *more intriguing* path appeared.

Tuning in to the field shifts our energy from force to flow—from pushing through life to consciously sensing, interpreting, and moving with the subtle energetic cues around and within us. I had some reservations, but deep down, I knew it was time to leap. When the opportunity came, it felt like an unmistakable nudge: equal parts exhilarating and terrifying. Once I committed and gave it my best effort, everything began to align. After years of grinding, things unfolded without force. Every step felt supported—the timing, the conversations, even my own confidence. The current I had been trying to outswim carried me forward with ease.

Surrender is not weakness; it is understanding that control is an illusion and that the most profound shifts happen when we allow life to unfold rather than force it into submission.

We develop Energetic Intelligence through the embodied practice of tuning in to inner and outer signals with objectivity, discerning ego from higher guidance to shift from force to flow and navigate life connected, intuitive, and aligned.

A few years later, navigating the unrelenting pace of corporate Amazon while healing from complex-PTSD became an overlapping journey that tested every part of my resilience, self-awareness, and capacity I had to lead—both myself and others.

But each experience offered the opportunity to consciously meet the fragmented parts of myself from a new state of awareness and transmute internal dissonance in real time. I began building Energetic Intelligence—the ability to sense, interpret, and respond to energetic and emotional data in real time. Recalibration begins with energetic awareness; in practice, it asks us to trust in something greater than ourselves.

---

**WHERE ENQ HELPS US MANAGE THE ENERGY WE CAN SENSE AND MEASURE, SPIRITUAL INTELLIGENCE (SQ) INVITES US TO SURRENDER TO GUIDANCE WE CANNOT FULLY EXPLAIN BUT CAN DEEPLY FEEL. TOGETHER THEY BRIDGE INNER ALIGNMENT AND TRUST IN THE UNSEEN—FAITH IN TIMING, MEANING, AND THE LARGER FIELD OF LIFE ITSELF.**

---

Trust and surrender quiet the noise, open the channel, and allow the brain and body to shift into harmony with the field—where signals arrive and action flows with certainty. In this state, you stop forcing, start listening, and act from the quiet conviction that you're exactly where you need to be. Research shows that during meditation or energy activation, the brain shifts into a unified state where insight can emerge without effort. Trust becomes a steady channel for guidance, aligning inner awareness with the field's intelligence.[26]

Belief is an act of self-leadership. It determines how we interpret the past, engage with the present, and create the future. It allows us to step outside of survival mode and into possibility. It shifts our nervous system from hypervigilance to expansion.

Neuroscience also supports this, demonstrating that our belief systems directly influence our physiological responses, cognitive flexibility, and ability to navigate adversity. *The Relaxation Response* found that letting go of control reduces cortisol, inflammation, and nervous system hyperarousal—shifting the body from fight-or-flight to flow, a critical skill for tuning in to the field. *The Surrender Experiment* reinforces this idea: the more we trust and stop micromanaging life, the more opportunities seem to unfold naturally.[27]

Faith—whether in yourself, your people, or the greater forces guiding your life—allows you to lead, create, and expand without burning out. For years, I resisted surrender. It felt like giving up, like losing control, like admitting defeat. What I didn't realize was that surrender isn't about passivity; it's about alignment.

Resonance is not about choosing between science and spirituality—it's recognizing they're the same conversation. Energy is real, belief is powerful, and the way we perceive the world shapes what is possible. Belief in something beyond ourselves—a higher power, the interconnectedness of life, or Quantum Intelligence—anchors us. It gives meaning to suffering, transforms obstacles into lessons, and allows us to move beyond the limitations of fear, control, and self-doubt into trust, surrender, and expansion.

Most importantly, it reconnects us to the energy that connects us all.

**True surrender isn't the absence of action; it's the release of resistance.**

Surrender is letting the field work *with* and *through* you.

It is knowing when to engage, act, observe, or step away. Over and over again, I gave people and places too many chances—my mom, my high school boyfriend, even Amazon. Surrender taught me the difference between holding space for growth, and draining my energy where alignment would never come.

In traditional spirituality, faith is trust in the unseen or surrender to divine timing. The same is true in quantum science and energetics. In leadership, this becomes inner steadiness, clarity under pressure, presence that models calm in conflict, and the ability to hold boundaries and expectations while creating psychological safety for others.

Like many others, my introduction to faith was through organized religion. Christianity, specifically. I hesitate to say I was raised Christian, due to the hypocrisy of the adults around me. I never viewed them, let alone myself, as Christian. I was in Awana, went to a Catholic school in kindergarten, and received a promise ring as I was "coming of age," despite an inner knowing that I was already "compromised."

I had conflicting feelings about my trust in the divine. But from a young age, I always felt an energetic presence, a palpable all-knowing, all-being consciousness. Faith isn't passive; it is alignment in action, trusting the field while tuning your own signal—an active exchange between your inner state and the field that informs your choices in real time.

## THE MODALITY OR MESSENGER IS UP TO YOU—WHAT MATTERS IS YOUR WILLINGNESS TO LISTEN AND RESPOND

Energetic Intelligence bridges your inner guidance with the signals in the field. From this space, you can see beyond old projections and patterns, respond with clarity, and act from integrity instead of pressure. When your nervous system and the field are in resonance, guidance flows naturally. You're no longer pushing—you're sensing, interpreting, and aligning with the moment. The deeper truth guiding both your actions and your impact becomes clear, and your decisions carry the invitation of alignment rather than the strain of control.

Belief is the energetic bridge between tuning in and acting in alignment. It converts inner coherence into the trust required to follow quantum signals, even in uncertainty. When we believe—deeply—in our vision, our value, and the greater field we're connected to, that belief shifts our frequency. It creates a steady internal resonance that others can feel, respond to, and align with.

The ability to trust in something greater than our immediate circumstances transforms fear and resistance into clarity and confident authority—especially when the systems around us suggest we shrink or play by outdated rules.

**Energetic recalibration is the catalyst for transformation—translating inner attunement into real, sustainable change.**

At Amazon, every challenge became an opportunity to pursue wholeness. Every healing breakthrough became an opportunity to lead differently, to clarify and model my own signal while more accurately interpreting the field's.

My intensity had always been my edge. I was relentless, focused, praised for getting results, but as I pushed against the system—against people's comfort zones—I was repeatedly told I was *too intense, too direct, too much.*

That tension made me pause and observe longer before stepping in, until one experience made the cost of ignoring myself unmistakably clear. During the COVID-19 pandemic, I was leading an inventory transition for 750-plus sites across the US and EU, when a peer leader asked me not to join a supplier call. He claimed he didn't want to "overwhelm them with too many Amazon reps."

I felt inner friction immediately—my body knew something was off—but I agreed anyway, afraid of being seen as difficult or domineering.

That decision put the entire project at risk; a critical delay in inventory supply followed. I felt it coming, but I'd lost time to communicate or pivot as I silenced myself to preserve harmony with others.

This was a key turning point. I began to trust friction as information, and aligned action as responsibility. I committed to no longer playing nice at the expense of what I knew to be right.

Energetic intelligence is trusting the feedback loop between your own coherence and the environment you're operating in. The more attuned you are to your internal signals, the more precisely you can read a system's readiness, resistance, and points of leverage.

When we change internally, we shift the environments around us. When we heal, we create space for others to do the same. When we trust friction as a signal for growth, misalignment becomes an invitation for repair. With undeniable accuracy, the field shows us exactly where and how to return to coherence.

I've never been one to "stay in my lane" or accept the status quo. From building entirely new functions and scaling mechanisms in record time, to holding a mirror up to the unspoken inefficiencies across teams, I learned to listen beyond what was said. Friction taught me that alignment isn't about shrinking to fit someone else's comfort; it's about discerning the difference between relational attunement and self-abandonment.

**Their discomfort wasn't about me. It was about what my conviction and Inner Authority activated in them.**

I was actively reshaping what leadership looked and felt like. My presence confronted the norms that others were used to. I could feel the friction—not just in tone or facial expressions but in my body. It was the same felt tension I now recognize as a signal that something deeper is misaligned. The annual review process became another data point, a feedback loop, each cycle affirming not only my capacity to create order from chaos but the perception ranges experienced by leaders, peers, and direct reports. I realized I wasn't being asked to shrink—I was being filtered through their fragmentation.

**When you cultivate a regulated inner guidance system, a balanced energy field, and an intentional approach to life, you become a more effective leader and change maker.**

I've always been justice-oriented, with an almost reflexive pull toward intervening. When I see patterns of inequity, manipulation, or harm, I step in. The problem is, sometimes I step in before others are ready to receive what I have to say. I've learned to look for patterns before engaging, but when they're clear, I expect people to "get it"—fast. When they don't, my patience frays. I get frustrated, and my energy spirals into misalignment and burnout.

These aren't my proudest moments, but the reality is that I have a low tolerance for inaction when stakes are high, and that's something I actively work to temper. Slowing down, conserving energy for receptive people and meaningful dialogue, while letting some fires burn without me. It's an ongoing practice to notice the early signals, pace my engagement, and recalibrate before stepping in so I can lead from composure, not misplaced urgency.

**COHERENCE IS CONTAGIOUS**

Nearly two years since my last SGB injection, I've learned to honor my body's signals rather than fight against them. I've built a life that works for me. I know when I need to recalibrate or create space for recovery. That awareness has allowed me to manage my nervous system, regulate my autoimmune symptoms, and maintain my health. Faith and surrender stabilize the nervous system, creating conditions for recalibration—where the brain and body return to coherence, and your frequency shifts from constriction to expansion.

When we're coherent within ourselves, we bring clarity and presence into interactions. Friction with others becomes an opportunity for mutual growth rather than a trigger for defense or disconnection. Our steadiness can help regulate the space, inviting the other person's system toward balance.

Community is the field where activation and repair happen most powerfully, because alignment builds the trust and stability needed for collective progress. The timing of our response to friction determines its impact and integration. Act too soon, and we risk reacting from ego; wait too long, and the opportunity for recalibration may pass.

Transformation accelerates in spaces where aligned individuals can mirror regulation, hold compassionate boundaries, and model new ways of responding to the unique challenges and complexity we face today.

In an era of social media, rising disenchantment with existing power structures, and Gen Z entering the workforce, authority is shifting. People no longer respond solely to positional power but to resonance, coherence, and integrity. Leadership is less about power; it is about what your presence activates in the system, and whether you can hold that activation long enough to allow for something new to emerge.

Spiritual Intelligence, Emotional Intelligence, and Energetic Intelligence: together, create discernment—the wisdom of aligned action. Alignment isn't static; it's a living state that strengthens every time you choose coherence over self-betrayal. The more you honor that state, the more naturally your actions reflect your values, your leadership embodies your purpose, and your presence becomes the invitation for others to rise.

**The Intelligence Triad:** Spiritual, emotional, and energetic intelligences form a dynamic triad that underpins conscious leadership. When these dimensions are integrated, leaders access both clarity and discernment, pairing intuitive insight with grounded action. This balance creates coherence between what we feel, think, and do.

Quantum Leadership requires leading from inner alignment and coherence, translating what you sense in the field into shared vision—so the right people, opportunities, and solutions naturally converge.

When leaders operate from internal coherence, resonance shows up as discernment over reaction, and grounded integrity over performance. Energetic alignment allows leaders to operate from authentic authority—especially when outcomes are unknown and stakes are high. Without it, responses give way to reactivity, and coherence fragments.

When certainty fades or distortion enters your field, internal resonance is what holds your frequency steady.

**Recalibration is the bridge between personal clarity and external courage.**

## BLINK

After my stepdad gets out of prison, his "mom" offers to let us live with her while he's on house arrest.

*I don't think it was actually his mom. I don't know who she was.*

He and my mom take over the garage at this lady's house, renovating it into a third bedroom. My brother and I share a den, or previous office space. It's cramped, even for two small children. I sleep on an old army cot, with a sleeping bag.

I can still hear the sound of canvas creaking and the melody of *Drift Away* in my mind.

Comforting me with hope for another life, as I try to end this one, digging deeper into my wrist.

## BLINK

Nine or ten? My mom and her husband—I *think* they're married by this time—end up on rocky ground again.

*Go figure. Meth will do that to you.*

They decide to split up. After some couch surfing, my mom moves us into an apartment in Sumner. We're living with my mom's "sister" at first, then my mom gets a job as the apartment manager and we move into a three-bedroom apartment.

*I hoped this was the part where things would turn around.*

## BLINK

Life is decent for a minute. But I begin to not trust these moments of reprieve. Before long, things will change. Her addiction gets bad again. I know when she's using, because I have to manage her schedule, wake her up to take us to school and get herself ready for work. But mostly I know because she frequently locks herself in her room. Or, when her "friends" come over, we're locked in our rooms. At some point she decides she needs to save money, and we move to a smaller two-bedroom apartment. Things get even worse after that.

*Uncertainty and chaos was the only certainty.*

# THE LEADERSHIP SHIFT

*"Leadership is about creating a domain in which human beings continually deepen their understanding of reality and become more capable of participating in the unfolding of the world. Ultimately, leadership is about creating new realities."*

—JOSEPH JAWORSKI

The way we lead others is a direct reflection of how we lead ourselves, and that begins with our own coherence. What you don't resolve internally, you will re-create endlessly in others. Unresolved wounds don't stay buried; they shape how we navigate relationships, careers, and our role within the broader collective.

We've been taught to define leadership through outcomes: team size, results, visibility, influence, prestige. But impact is not determined by your strategic prowess or tactical skill set—it is determined by your energy. When leaders set a tone of trust, courage, and resilience, they entrain systems through their own energetic coherence—disrupting the very systems that penalize presence, collaboration, and discernment—especially for women and nonconformers.

## LEADERS SET THE ENERGETIC TONE FOR AN ORGANIZATION—CONSCIOUSLY OR UNCONSCIOUSLY

Leadership is not about forcing outcomes but about embodying alignment—where presence itself becomes the strategy. It is found in the ability to lead with clarity and coherence, qualities that emerge only when we commit to doing the inner work. Quantum Leadership, whether personal or organizational, requires the courage to hold space for both the pain of the present and the possibility of the future.

A leader who operates from coherence rather than chaos can diffuse tension, navigate uncertainty with grace, and elevate the collective energy of a team or organization.

Great leaders don't just inspire with words—they influence through energy.

I've held nearly every kind of power a corporate system can give you: title, authority, and expanded scope. None of those ever made me feel safe or whole. In fact most of them offered the opposite, a requirement to prove, perform, and push the limits of my own character—my own values and ethics.

It wasn't until I redefined leadership in my own mind as an *energetic imprint*—not a role—that I finally understood what power actually is.

It's not force. It's frequency.

When wielded by leaders who are internally aligned, it can be shared and used for collective benefit, offering each of us the opportunity to transform ourselves and the world we live in. When the opposite is true, the cost is a systemic cycle of misalignment that depletes individuals while sustaining unhealthy expectations.

Burnout is not a personal failure; it is a system-driven phenomenon designed to extract the maximum output from individuals while convincing us that exhaustion is a sign of personal failure. Overwork has been glorified as a status symbol, trapping individuals in cycles of exhaustion while corporations reap the benefits.

**Burnout is prolonged misalignment—a disconnect between personal well-being and systemic expectations.**

At the height of my career, I was living in deep incongruence between who I was and who the role expected me to be. Like many women in leadership, I wasn't just navigating deliverables and life outside of work. I was navigating role congruity bias—the unspoken pressure to perform competence and warmth, authority and modesty, confidence and approachability, strength and selflessness.

Women in leadership consistently outperform traditional hierarchical models by integrating collaboration, empathy, and leadership practices that sustain people and performance. Rosabeth Moss Kanter's studies found that companies with gender-diverse leadership are better equipped to navigate crises, drive long-term profitability, and create inclusive workplace cultures.[28] Women-led businesses tend to foster psychological safety, continuous learning, and resilience—factors that enable adaptability in an increasingly volatile world. Yet role congruity theory explains that women are penalized when their leadership style doesn't conform to traditional gender expectations.[29]

This reinforces systemic burnout by invalidating authentic expression and eroding psychological safety. This is not just a workplace issue; it is deeply tied to societal expectations. Gender roles and conditioning create rigid expectations, pushing people to reject the parts of themselves that don't conform. Shame-based conditioning forces people to internalize wounds instead of processing them, leading to generations of unaddressed denial and pain.

The social role theory explains how gender expectations are shaped by societal structures rather than innate differences.[30] Yet gender norms dictate behaviors in leadership, relationships, and personal expression, reinforcing self-suppression for the sake of acceptance. Girls are conditioned to be agreeable, nurturing, and emotionally accommodating. Boys are taught that emotional vulnerability is weakness, leading to suppression and isolation. Both experience conditioning that creates dissonance between their true nature and what is deemed socially acceptable. The gender schema theory further supports this, showing that we internalize cultural expectations of masculinity and femininity from an early age, shaping the templates we use to evaluate who looks and feels like a leader.[31]

Growing up, I received conflicting messages about what it meant to be a woman. Like most young girls, I was bombarded with rules about how to exist. I learned early on to be a "good girl," obedient, polite, accommodating.

I hated that requirement. I resented the idea that softness meant weakness.

I played football at recess all the way through middle school, convinced I would've been a decent wide receiver had I not stopped growing in sixth grade. I was a tomboy, all the way through early high school.

I saw my mother and the women around me shrink themselves in relationships, enduring mistreatment, compromising their needs, sacrificing their dignity. I blamed them for it. I loathed the idea of being a "good girl" because I equated it with submission, passivity, and self-abandonment—traits that erased competence rather than honored it.

Instead, I became a "tough girl," a "take no shit" girl—determined to never let anyone mistake my strength for weakness. But in doing so, I rejected my own depth and my ability to receive and trust quantum signals.

This created dissonance in my field. I was projecting strength while internally battling disconnection. The energetic cost of suppressing half of myself was immense—a daily denial that compounded with every misaligned decision and action.

> **TO BE CLEAR, THIS IS NOT JUST ABOUT GENDER; IT IS ABOUT HOW LEADERSHIP IS FUNDAMENTALLY DEFINED AND MEASURED. THE RESISTANCE TO FULLY INTEGRATE THESE MODELS IS NOT ABOUT EFFECTIVENESS. IT IS ABOUT DEEPLY INGRAINED POWER STRUCTURES THAT RESIST CHANGE.**

Regenerative transformation requires dismantling the outdated models and behaviors that prioritize individual competition over collective success—starting with how we show up and lead every day. For many, transformation requires unlearning these prescribed roles, releasing the parts of ourselves we were taught to suppress, and reclaiming Inner Authority.

At Amazon, every signal distortion, protective pattern, and unprocessed activation became an opportunity to lead myself from fragmentation into confident alignment. Over the years, my leadership evolution has been both intentional and quantum in nature—each chapter layering new frequencies of insight, responsibility, and depth.

The problems I walked into were messy and urgent, exactly the kind of chaos I learned to organize as a child. My superpower was creating order and executing under fire. I became known for my ability to turn teams around quickly, push boundaries, and deliver results. I moved through Operations, FBA, Customer Service, HR, Supply Chain, IT, and Community Operations—each transition marking both a career milestone and a deeper layer of personal transformation.

The roles got bigger, the pressure mounted.

**My external experiences began to mirror fractures and necessary recalibration within my internal world.**

I knew how to get results, but the pace left no room to breathe—high standards without grace, momentum without restoration. For the first few years of my career, I wasn't transforming people or systems at all. I was merely managing my own survival.

Feedback surfaced that my standards left some people feeling intimidated or demoralized. My growing edge became clearer with every experience. One mentor finally said what few would, "No one can meet your standards but you." They were right. I have relentlessly high expectations. Some people rose with me and grew; others couldn't keep pace.

What we don't heal, we inevitably hand down to others. Fragmented leaders can unintentionally perpetuate dysfunction under the guise of performance—often without realizing how they're contributing to or creating the problem.

Some leaders met my clarity with trust and expansion, encouraging my growth beyond their own readiness. Others retreated into control and fear. This contrast forced me to clarify my own energetic signature and choose coherence over compliance—anchoring my leadership not in pleasing others but in embodying the field I wanted to cultivate around me.

While leading a team of about three hundred people, and shortly after I began unraveling my own fragmentation, I ran straight into a wall of friction. My direct leader lied compulsively, convincing me that my L7 promotion had been approved and she was renegotiating my salary increase.

It hadn't been, and she wasn't.

When I brought the issue to my director, she was dismissive, defensive, and emotionally checked out. She scoffed at each concern I raised and example I provided. To me, that moment clarified that the system isn't just flawed. It is *intentionally upheld*—consciously or unconsciously.

After taking a sabbatical in 2021 to prioritize my health, I gained clarity on my purpose and unique value. I decided I would stay at Amazon only for an opportunity with a clear path to promotion. After two in less than three years, and then four successive years of top performance ratings, I thought I was long overdue.

Then another moment of resistance.

I had been chasing my L7 promotion, the last level prior to Executive (L8+), since the mishandling in 2017. When I had the opportunity to interview for an L7 role, the hiring manager told me they'd have to down-level the role in order to pursue my promotion doc *after* joining the organization. This meant they would bring me into the organization to do the L7 role as an L6 because that was my current level. Despite understanding the process, every trauma response in my body lit up.

My nervous system knew what it was like to be promised things that never materialized.

The old me would've spiraled. Overperformed. Overexplained my worth and readiness.

In the space between stimulus and response—the zero point— we decide whether or not to act in accordance with who we say we are, or who we're becoming. The space where our choices determine the unfolding of events.

There is a version of me that would've panicked. Tried to control the outcome. Overcompensated. Anything to avoid being burned again. That version was born in the early years of my life and my career, especially in roles where I had been lied to, passed over, promised things that never came, and discarded by people and systems that rewarded compliance over courage.

But I didn't spiral. I didn't panic. I trusted the alignment of the moment, the frequency, and the field that brought this opportunity to my reality.

I let go of desperation and replaced it with discernment—constantly assessing my actions, behaviors, and energetic frequency against what I began to notice coming from others. This clarity and confidence in my path allowed me to enter that position authentically—anchored.

I didn't abandon attunement. I just stopped letting fear hold the mic.

I changed.

Instead of panicking, I paused. Instead of grasping, I grounded.

*How was this moment illuminating a path I couldn't yet see or understand?*

*How could I use this moment to align my present self with my most aligned self?*

*How could this lead to my own evolution and the evolution of those around me?*

In addition to building a continuous improvement team and culture, I was offered an informal chief of staff role—great positioning to help lead large-scale cultural transformation. The role was critical to my career goals, regardless of the promotion. Leading organizational transformation for a global team of over 5,500 people was a defining opportunity that crystallized my path as an Organization Development practitioner, an interdisciplinary field focused on aligning people, culture, and systems to advance human-centered organizational excellence.

So I let go—releasing the need to control the outcome—and the promotion came within a few short months.

The following review cycle, after eight years and three promotions, I received my first "Meets High Bar" rating, as opposed to "Exceeds" as I'd become accustomed to. However, my manager only mentioned one LP opportunity—and simultaneously noted that I was seen as a role model of Amazon's Leadership Principles.

Being commended as a role model while receiving my lowest rating to date created a cognitive and energetic dissonance I couldn't ignore. My initial concern was that the feedback and my overall impact on the organization didn't match the rating I was given. Once I was told it was because of the default promotion rating, my secondary concern became the role congruity theory—which explores how stereotypes about gender and leadership influence valuations of competence and fit.

*If I were a man, would we be having different conversations right now?*

That tension between being told I was a role model while receiving the lowest rating I'd ever received magnified the inner work I was doing: learning to reclaim my voice and refusing to diminish my power while calling attention to contradictory systems.

I tried to understand the inconsistency in my rating, the feedback I was receiving, and the efficacy with which I had predicted organizational failure points. My directness about inefficiencies, layoffs, and team dynamics was often disregarded—until it became undeniable.

Again and again, I found myself in the tension between my own authenticity and others' comfort. I wasn't just asking them to deploy a specific strategy; I was asking them to reconsider what effective leadership looks like. It took time (and humility) to understand that their hesitation wasn't resistance—it was disorientation.

Friction isn't rejection. It is just feedback, an invitation to slow down, tune in, and evolve together.

This is the cost of rigid, command-and-control cultures: emotions and humanity are often checked at the door. They demand compliance, suppression, and disconnection from reality. We shrink, presenting a sanitized, palatable version of ourselves for the comfort of those around us—at the expense of our wholeness, our authenticity, and internal alignment. We become disconnected from ourselves, our teams, and our work.

---

**DESPITE THE OVERWHELMING EVIDENCE SUPPORTING HUMAN-CENTERED LEADERSHIP, THE STRUCTURES THAT DOMINATE POLITICAL, CORPORATE, AND ECONOMIC SYSTEMS ACTIVELY RESIST THIS TRANSFORMATION.**

---

Traditional business models have long perpetuated the false dichotomy between profit and people, operating from the belief that financial success must come at the expense of employee well-being. Economic models that value people over profit reinforce systemic inequalities that prevent widespread human flourishing.

Rutger Bregman's research in *Humankind* debunks the myth that human nature is inherently competitive, arguing that society has been *conditioned* to prioritize individual gain over collective good.[32] This is reinforced by Mariana Mazzucato's work in *The Value of Everything*, which highlights how traditional economic models undervalue caregiving, education, and community work. Kate Raworth's *Doughnut Economics* challenges the notion that infinite economic growth is the ultimate goal, advocating instead for regenerative models that balance human well-being with sustainability. Robert D. Putnam's *Bowling Alone* furthers this conversation by showing that declining civic engagement and increasing social fragmentation contribute to a collective leadership crisis.

Similarly, Frederic Laloux's work on Teal Organizations highlights how decentralized, human-centered leadership creates resilient, adaptive organizations that thrive even in uncertain environments.[33] In contrast to traditional hierarchical models that rely on rigid control and bureaucracy, Teal Organizations are structured around self-management, purpose-driven leadership, and evolutionary adaptability—allowing businesses to evolve organically rather than being stifled by outdated, over-utilized command-and-control structures.

Leadership must evolve beyond short-term individual gain toward long-term societal impact. Leaders who continue to measure success solely by profit margins inevitably create systems that exploit rather than uplift. If organizations and governments fail to integrate human-centered economic models, they will continue to contribute to disconnection, economic disparity, and systemic dysfunction. This is not about abandoning capitalism; it is about redesigning our systems to work for people rather than against them.

Shoshana Zuboff's research in *The Age of Surveillance Capitalism* exposes how digital platforms manipulate human behavior for profit, eroding personal agency and reinforcing consumer dependency.[34] *Manufacturing Consent*, by Edward S. Herman and Noam

Chomsky, explains how media and political systems are structured to maintain power dynamics that discourage systemic change.[35] The goal is not to foster independent thinkers; it is to maintain hierarchical control through misinformation, fear, and distraction.

## LEADERSHIP IS NOT JUST ABOUT INTELLECT, TACTICS, OR STRATEGY—IT IS ABOUT THE ENERGY WE BRING INTO EVERY SPACE WE ENTER

I've worked under leaders who modeled trust, vision, and accountability. Some leaders encouraged self-awareness and set high standards. Others took time to recognize how our work contributed to shared goals. One leader gave me my first program management opportunity, believed in my vision, and supported my growth. When I brought up a new approach or strategy, they asked thoughtful questions, then trusted me to execute. Even when they didn't fully understand the path, they provided the space, resources, and guidance to grow. In HR and Supply Chain, leaders made space for people's strengths to flourish. And in OTS, I was initially given room to run, illuminating how personal transformation and self-transcendence naturally expand into collective service, directly shaping team and business outcomes. Their clarity wasn't attachment. They didn't grip tightly. They created conditions for others to lead powerfully. Their belief made me braver. More honest. More effective.

I've also worked under leaders who couldn't hold that frequency—in FBA, Customer Service, OTS, and CommOps. Every ethical and leadership failure demonstrated what happens when coherence, clarity, and resonance is replaced with control, insecurity, or comparison. When I pushed for growth and excellence, they hesitated. Doubted. Withheld. When I asked tough questions, they responded by tightening oversight, doubling down on process, or reassigning key responsibilities without explanation.

Rather than get curious, they grew defensive. They stopped

inviting me to key meetings and offered surface-level engagement while quietly undermining my influence.

My clarity and conviction revealed their discomfort. My confidence clashed with their fragility. Instead of trusting what was possible, they clung to what was familiar.

Power. Compliance. Comfort.

**Leadership is rapidly becoming less about what you do—and more about who you are and the frequency you transmit.**

In OTS, when a new director came along, clearly not a fan of my proposal for a team merge, he shut down the conversation in the middle of my recommendation. "Just stop calling it that," he blurted out. "We're not doing it!"

I had already made tremendous progress in gaining buy-in from key stakeholders prior to his arrival. I stayed in harmony with the field, preserving my energy and frequency for showing up fully in the present, where the real value is created and possibility lies. That detachment became my leverage. I wasn't chasing their approval. I was building what I *knew* was needed. That energy shifted everything, from how I created the team and developed strategy to how I earned trust with key stakeholders—ultimately facilitating successful cultural transformation in one of Amazon's most complex organizations.

I took the challenge on, confident it was right for customers, employees, and the business. I sought support and advice from other key leaders. Unfortunately, most seemed preoccupied with their own political and positional standing. My own boss deflected with passive comments and superficial engagement. I rarely asked for help, but I needed extra support to navigate challenges that he could *easily* influence by simply setting the right standard through his own behavior. Instead, he shrugged it off by saying he faced similar issues—failing to recognize how gender roles and positional authority made those challenges fundamentally different for me.

Like I did while growing up, I charged ahead for as long as

I possibly could. First, focusing on my own opportunities for growth. I made progress initially, gaining strong buy-in from ground-level folks. But exclusionary behavior quickly pulled me back into doubt, reminding me that my true leverage begins internally—in personal authority and energetic frequency.

Eventually, after compiling a growing list of examples, I spoke with the specific individuals who said or did the most concerning things, and requested that they adjust their behavior. While uncomfortable for all, my goal was to handle things as constructively as I possibly could, while still owning my truth and standing in my power.

When change didn't come quickly enough, my impatience and relentlessly high standards for leadership led me to a quick conversation with the VP about my observations and concerns. In response, she gave her own example, then looked at me and said, "You just have to take your power back."

I was pissed. *What do you mean?* I thought. *I'm here, telling you what the problem is, how you can fix it, AND how I can help.*

Take my power back?

I already had. Just not in the way she meant. She wanted me to grin and bear it, wait my turn, play nice—the same BS I'd been hearing from those above me for years.

Standing in my power demanded that I speak up.

I was in such a powerful state, and had clarity in having the hard conversation because I had taken the time to thoughtfully reflect on and assess my perception, and their potential blind spots, before engaging. I also left the door open for reparative dialogue. The VP had it wrong. By being there, having the conversation, I *was* standing in my power.

**I finally understood what it meant to lead from Inner Authority, not overcompensation.**

For the first time, I stopped trying to *out-logic* the dysfunction.

I trusted my felt sense. My knowing.

My Energetic Intelligence.

**Every person has a frequency. A tone. A felt presence.**

The future of leadership isn't about control; it's about liberation.

The question isn't whether transformation is possible. The question is whether leaders are ready to step into their roles as architects of a better system.

Energetic coherence in leadership is the quiet, immovable conviction that you're not here to chase; you're here to *be*. It's detaching from someone else's expectations and demands, and standing firmly in your integrity.

It's leading from your aligned frequency, not your inherited fear.

Whether we're conscious of it or not, we're constantly influencing—and being influenced by—the energy around us. When you've done the work to heal, regulate, and align, your presence carries a steadiness others can feel.

Past conditioning influences our choices, until self-awareness leads to transformation. Leadership is an extension of coherence and Inner Authority. Those who do the work to heal, break cycles, and lead beyond the self are not just transforming themselves—they are shaping the future.

When we align with human-centered values, our leadership naturally shifts from transactional to transformational. We move beyond performative optics into authentic, embodied impact and collective contribution—the felt resonance that inspires and transforms others.

Coherence and alignment exist in continuous dialogue. As our inner coherence deepens, we embody greater alignment with our external actions and choices. In turn, practicing alignment reinforces and refines inner coherence, creating a self-sustaining cycle of integrity and growth.

Coherence refers to the *state* within—the integration and energetic harmony between your thoughts, emotions, and actions. Alignment refers to how that inner coherence *expresses outwardly*—your actions, decisions, and energetic imprint matching your inner truth.

They are both a result *and* a feedback loop. As you build inner coherence, you naturally move into greater alignment. As you practice alignment, you strengthen inner coherence.

Leaders who lack energetic stability and resonance can't create safety. They can't hold space for potential because they're still protecting their own fragility. Eventually, that fragmentation becomes cultural—buried in performance reviews, hiring and head count decisions, intentional omissions, and unspoken hierarchies.

## QUANTUM LEADERSHIP IS BUILT ON THE FOUNDATION OF INNER AUTHORITY, STEMMING FROM OUR OWN INNER TRANSFORMATION

When discussing personal transformation, most people think of Maslow's hierarchy of needs, but Carl Rogers offered an equally influential lens. He viewed self-actualization as a journey of congruence—aligning the real self, perceived self, and ideal self. Similar to the message in this book, Rogers emphasized ongoing alignment between who we are, how we see ourselves, and who we're becoming.[36]

When leaders cultivate coherence—a physiological state where the heart, brain, and nervous system are in sync—they enhance not only their own clarity and resilience but also the emotional stability of those around them. A leader's heart rhythm influences the nervous systems of their team, beyond verbal or nonverbal communication.

Alignment is the state of acting in accordance with your values, your truth, and your inner knowing—consistently and courageously. Coherence is the tone of your Inner Authority that influences how your actions land. Resonance occurs when that coherence harmonizes with others, creating collective stability and trust.

Energetic Intelligence is the capacity to sense, interpret, and align with this energy. That awareness is the energetic foundation of Quantum Leadership.

To help illuminate these dynamics, I've developed the Quantum Leadership Quadrant—integrating energetic frequency, intelligence, and authority—to assess the external impact of internal resistance, recalibration, and growth. It is grounded in Organization Development, leadership, and coaching practices across industries ranging from global tech to emergent startups. Building on systems thinking, adult development, somatics, and neuroscience, it supports emerging insights that position Energetic Intelligence as a vital skill for navigating relational dynamics and organizational impact.

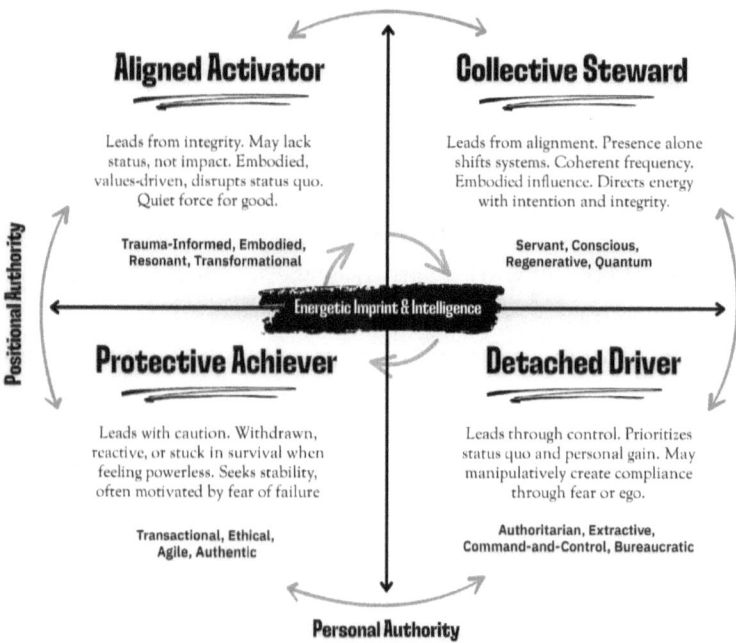

**Quantum Leadership Quadrant:** It's important to note that coherence, power, and alignment are interpreted differently across cultural contexts and that fragmentation has many origins—from trauma to conditioning. This framework serves as a map for navigating toward alignment. It is best used as a guide for orientation and personal reflection.

As shown, leadership emerges through the interaction of three distinct dimensions: Personal Authority (inner alignment, integrity, self-trust), Positional Authority (influence, power, relational impact), and Energetic Frequency and Intelligence (the degree of alignment between one's inner truth and outward behavior). This is your ability to sense and manage self while responding to external demands with intentionality, and the felt sense others with EnQ discern based on congruence between actions and felt presence.

Energetic Intelligence influences how both forms of authority are leveraged—determining whether power is expressed from fear and control or from coherence and service.

Together, this illustrates how energy, integrity, and influence converge to shape a leader's immediate and long-term impact. Through personal transformation and energetic recalibration, leaders may evolve from survival-based or control-driven modes (Protective Achiever and Detached Driver) toward expanded capacity for embodied, resonant impact (Aligned Activator and Collective Steward). Quantum Leadership arises from embodied inner alignment—an energetic foundation that precedes strategy, informs presence, and shapes every interaction. Quantum Leadership becomes accessible through ethical principles, servant focus, and a desire to lead positive change to benefit all.

This visual invites you to reflect not only on how you lead but from where—the coherence of your inner world, the integrity of your energy, and the frequency you carry. It's a map for moving from transactional influence to quantum, regenerative leadership: the kind that transforms systems simply through your energetic signature. It's a practical, repeatable method for aligning your inner state with your external influence, and developing shared vision through a system's lens. It bridges what is seen and unseen—inner alignment and outer impact, personal truth and collective design.

The more aligned you are, the more naturally your leadership becomes a force for coherence, collective clarity, progress, and growth. The more misaligned you are, the more your leadership—no matter how polished—creates instability, mistrust, and fear.

**Integrating your fragmented parts isn't just for personal benefit—it's a leadership imperative.**

When a leader is fragmented or forceful, they can pull the room into incoherence, but when they are grounded, regulated, and centered, they create an invisible but measurable field of stability—one that fosters trust, engagement, and expansion.

Studies on heart–brain coherence show that one person's regulated rhythm can physiologically entrain others into greater stability. Recalibrating your own energetic frequency is essential. You can't lead others into wholeness if you're still leading from your wounds.

Recalibration is how you stop mistaking control for clarity and projecting survival patterns onto your team. You learn to create spaces where people don't just perform but thrive.

In leadership, people's systems naturally gravitate toward the most dominant or powerful energy in the room—but when coherence is present, they attune to that signal instead. When grounded, regulated, and aligned, you become the stabilizing force others unconsciously match.

In my last role at Amazon with Community Operations, I was functioning from a completely different energetic frequency. Intentionally trying to transform the system, I brought up Peter Senge's *The Fifth Discipline*. I spoke about organizational health. I pushed for strategic goals to create systemic impact. But the more I spoke, the more fragmented leaders avoided me. One director dismissed these conversations as "philosophical," while also acknowledging it was the second time the book had been recommended.

Quantum Leadership and systemic inspection looks like a threat to those who haven't done the internal work. Instead of meeting possibility with curiosity, they dismiss it as impossible or illogical, failing to sense the creative emergence begging to unfold.

In a system that rewards compliance and adherence to unspoken rules written by those who have navigated before us, we're taught to absorb dysfunction as personal failure instead of calling it out and displaying accountability to improve.

Once I stopped internalizing other people's behavior and energy, I learned to tune in to my own frequency, my own inner guidance, and my own operating system. *Was it my own distortion, or their destructive behavior?*

Sometimes it's both.

The world does not need more people pretending to be fine. It does not need more fake, forced comradery or bypassing. We need leaders who are emotionally and energetically intelligent. We need people who create space for the full range of human experiences. Leaders who understand that doing the deep personal work—recalibrating in alignment with their true self—increases not only coherence and presence but overall efficacy, empathy, and engagement.

**True leadership is an energetic force.**

Leadership is about creating space for real, raw conversations, fostering emotional intelligence, and ensuring that people feel psychologically safe enough to express dissent, frustration, and growth opportunities.

The most effective leaders create space for truth and reconciliation. When leaders suppress dissent, avoid difficult conversations, or prioritize "keeping the peace" over healthy conflict, they create a culture of stagnation, resentment, and misalignment.[37] Avoiding discomfort becomes an insidious force in leadership—masquerading as optimism while suppressing creativity and co-creation.

**Real leaders don't avoid discomfort; they make room for it.**

The same internal fragmentation that distorts personal leadership mirrors the authoritarian patterns we see in failing systems—rigid, avoidant, and afraid of collective progress. To counter this, conscious, human-centered people must embrace a new model of leadership, one that welcomes uncomfortable truths, dissenting perspectives, and courageous vision.

Holding space for real, raw, human experiences is what leadership is truly about.

Personal transformation is the only way to provide this, first to yourself, then for others.

**Quantum Leaders create safety, expansion, and possibility—often without saying a word.**

They create the conditions where transformation becomes inevitable—where embodied Energetic Intelligence dissolves resistance, allowing growth and ideas to emerge naturally within and around us.

The work of tomorrow's leader is not to command; it is to *guide*. Not to impose their will but to create spaces where people feel safe enough to push the limits, heal, evolve, and lead themselves to new heights.

**Leadership is no longer strictly about hierarchy and dominance—it is about shared power, trust, and the ability to entrain the field.**

Bringing our whole selves into leadership requires deliberate action: developing emotional awareness, challenging inherited beliefs about power and success, leading with vulnerability rather than control, and creating environments where possibility thrives.

Quantum Leaders create space for the full spectrum of human experience, knowing that the most innovative ideas, the most radical growth, and the most meaningful transformation come not from comfort but from confronting what most would rather ignore.

Leaders who can't create safe, conscious, human-centered environments are failing the very people they're supposed to serve. When people feel valued, heard, and supported, engagement, innovation, and long-term profitability naturally increase.[38]

**Awareness sparks transformation. Personal transformation fuels collective evolution.**

Collective change requires leaders who are willing to disrupt the status quo, not just in thought but in action. Leaders must unlearn outdated models and redefine success through personal transformation and collective progress. Organizations must prioritize well-being, adaptability, and ethical leadership, and society must reject the notion that work defines worth and rebuild systems that support human flourishing.

Refusing to engage your own growth isn't leadership—it's complicity and a barrier. If you're not shifting the system, you're sustaining it, and missing the chance to create real change.

The work of reshaping leadership is inseparable from the work of reshaping the systems it operates within. When leaders embody coherence, self-awareness, and energetic alignment, they not only shift their own presence; they influence the structures around them.

The real question is not whether this shift is possible. It is whether we, the people in positions of power, have the courage to make it happen.

Quantum Leadership is personal alignment transforming into collective evolution. Quantum entrainment is the *mechanism*—systemic feature—for collective coherence. As more individuals raise their frequency and embody congruence, the collective field reaches a tipping point—an energetic shift that transforms relationships, teams, and systems.

Collective change starts with one.

**You.**

**BLINK**

Ten? Eleven? I'm so sick of my mom's shit. Of living like this. The house is filthy all the time. I'm tired of doing my own laundry, the dishes, reminding my mom to buy food and pay bills. Hoping and praying she won't forget us at school every day. A lot of times, I'm the last kid. She's deep in drug addiction. The selfishness and all-consuming nature of the high makes it impossible for her to think about, let alone consider her kids.

*Have you ever watched somebody who has been up for days try to keep themselves awake? Without their drugs, they fall asleep slowly. It's like a toddler trying to fight sleep at a table, with a plate of cake. With every nod-off, there's a startled response as they try to force themselves awake. It still makes me sick to my stomach.*

*Why couldn't she just be a better mom?*

**BLINK**

I think I'm eleven now. These idiots are so high out of their minds—tweaking, rushing around the apartment frantically. "Great, here we go again." I roll my eyes and walk back into my room, stepping over piles of unidentifiable filth.

They're anxious, rambunctious. "Where'd my fucking money go?" he yells.

Money? My interest was piqued. I didn't like this guy. His shorts, his tie-dyed tank tops and T-shirts. He was no hippie. He was a monster, and I saw it in him the first time I met him.

*If nothing else, this life gave me the gift of discernment.*

"Where's the money? Where's my money!" He's getting louder and angrier.

I decided to look around. I didn't have to look hard.

There it is, fifty bucks, sitting right there on top of the garbage can. I grab it slowly, put it in my pocket, act like I didn't see anything, and go back to my room to wait for things to calm down.

*The attention span of an addict is short and they live entirely reactionary.*

Something else will capture their attention soon enough and they'll leave. Once they do, so do we. I grab my brother from his room, wade through all the toys. No actual carpet in sight.

"Get your shoes, let's go." Our little feet take hurried steps up the driveway to the main road. We sit and wait. The bus comes regularly. I figure it'll come sooner or later.

I'm not anxious. I've become comfortable with independence. I've gotten comfortable being the one in charge. I prefer it when she isn't around.

The bus finally arrives. I drop in our fare, the weight of the driver's gaze getting heavier and heavier with each *tink, tink, tink, tink*. I smile at him, then quickly pull my brother to a seat nearby.

I'm cognizant of my surroundings. Another great skill I've acquired along the way. I can spot a dangerous person from a mile away. My heart, soul, and body language say, "don't fuck with me."

Thankfully, our stop isn't far. A couple minutes later, we jump off, just outside of the store. Walk swiftly in, grab a grocery cart, do a couple of laps around the store, get some food, a few weird looks, and then get on the bus and go home with our groceries.

*Nobody noticed anything. Nobody had any idea we even left.*

## BLINK

The house is a mess. My brother and I are hungry. Mom is passed out. Typical.

If we don't matter, what does? What will actually get her attention? What will she change for? Why won't she make a different choice?

I slide off my bed, fling the bedroom door open, then the bathroom door. Throw the closet shutter open, get on my tiptoes, and reach up to grab her meth bong.

Why is she choosing the drugs over us?!

I stomp through piles of laundry, past the washer and dryer she hasn't touched in weeks.

Fuck this. Fuck her.

I march over to the main office, just through the parking lot, turn the corner, go in the front door, and walk straight into her boss's office and slam the bong on her desk.

*I was done waiting for her to get better, to make better choices. Done hoping she would realize I needed her. I never regretted turning her in. I never wished I had stayed silent. The mother I wanted and the mother I got were never the same person. Her anger shaped my inner dialogue. For years, the voice in my head mirrored the sharpness of hers. The revolving door of men, the instability in father figures, the lack of relationship with my own.*

## BLINK

*You could say this was my first experience with unintended consequences.*

My brother and I are sleeping on the floor of a single-wide in Spokane. We've moved in with my aunt and uncle while my mom is in rehab.

It's better than foster care. Or the last time this happened. I'm grateful, but more than anything, I'm hopeful.

*Without any other way of processing, I internalized my mother's addiction as a personal failure or sign of unworthiness. The day I turned her in, I interrupted that encoding. That moment marked the reclamation of my voice—and I've been consciously unlearning the encoded frequencies originally given to me ever since.*

# PART TWO

# ALIGNMENT

Fragmentation is not a flaw. It's a natural response to a world that asks us to suppress our truth in exchange for survival. But the cost is high: it distorts our signal, clouds our decisions, and weakens our leadership.

Part One, traced how fragmentation affects choices, while exploring how presence, awareness, and Energetic Intelligence open the door to coherence—a foundation that allows us to see beyond survival and reclaim our unique value and purpose.

If we cannot recognize and respond to our own internal signals, we default to noise, distortion, and external pressures. Aligned action comes from learning to trust your blueprint—attuning to and flowing with the field.

In Part Two, we'll move deeper into that practice—shifting into alignment, reclaiming and learning to lead from your energetic signature. You will also be introduced to the frameworks that fuel my ongoing Personal and Organization Development practice. These tools emerged from thousands of hours of professional practice and lived experience as well as years of reflection and research on power, leadership, and personal transformation.

They're what I wish I'd had when I was in the thick of friction, conflict, and misalignment. My hope is that these tools will help you see where you are, sense where others are, and navigate conflict and resistance with clarity and conviction.

The path forward asks us to reclaim our Inner Authority—aligning mind, body, and soul into an integrated operating system, dissipating fragmented energy or reinforcing it through our actions. By regulating our internal network: brain, body, and energetic field, we access our inner guidance system, helping us respond to life from internal coherence and wholeness.

As you turn the page, you'll learn to embody this shift for yourself—to cultivate Inner Authority, awaken your Energetic Intelligence, align with your zero point, and ultimately activate your unique blueprint.

# GROWTH

>>>>>>>

ADDRESS SKILL, STRUCTURE, AND INTERPERSONAL GAPS

# INNER AUTHORITY

*"The soil of our mind contains many seeds, positive and negative. We are the gardeners who identify, water, and cultivate the best seeds."*
—THICH NHAT HANH

Trauma or rejection of our true self leads to fragmentation. Fragmentation distorts our signal. Inner Authority is how we reclaim our signal—so we can lead from aligned intention instead of immediate reaction.

*You aren't enough. You aren't worthy. You're unlovable.*

Lies. And yet we build our lives around them as core beliefs.

When we're activated, these old scripts play out. Inner Authority breaks that cycle.

Cultivating Inner Authority requires ongoing recalibration—the practice of tuning back in to coherence when external pressure, old patterns, or systemic forces pull us off-center. Discernment forces us to assess, *where did these beliefs come from?*

*Who taught me this? What experiences reinforced the message?*

And perhaps most importantly: *what is true?*

## INNER AUTHORITY IS QUIET CLARITY THAT EMERGES WHEN WE STOP OUTSOURCING OUR TRUTH

You can't lead others or calibrate external energy if your *internal system* is fragmented. To transform ourselves, we must build the skill of deciphering internal versus external distortion, Inner Authority versus our programming, and unresolved fragmentation versus overprotective ego. The alignment between your internal state (thoughts, beliefs, emotional regulation, energetic presence) and your external behaviors (decisions, communication, impact) creates coherence—the foundation of Quantum Leadership: the ability to lead through presence, clarity, and resonance.

Inner Authority is the capacity to discern and act from your purpose.

By reclaiming our Inner Authority, we cut through distortion and attune to the intelligence beyond ourselves, allowing us to move through friction, challenges, delays, and paths we didn't realize we wanted or needed to take for the bigger picture to come together.

**Leaders who have done the inner work lead differently.**

In nearly every transformational conversation I've had, the root cause of the challenge ultimately came down to one tension: the friction between what felt authentic and true, and what their environment demanded.

For years, I pushed. I achieved. Yet something felt unresolved. No matter how much I accomplished, I struggled under the emotional weight of my own trauma and conditioning. It took years of therapy, daily thought interruptions, and regular energy work to recognize that what I thought was strength was, in many ways, just well-disguised survival mechanisms.

Internal Family Systems (IFS) reiterates that unresolved trauma often leads to fragmentation of the self. Different parts of the psyche create protective mechanisms to avoid pain.[39] This occurs and is reinforced regularly in a world that constantly asks us to disconnect from ourselves and others.

The belief that worthiness is tied to external success: perfectionism.

A response to early betrayal or abandonment: hyper-independence.

A propensity to avoid uncertainty and chaos: control.

A way to prove worthiness and escape deeper wounds: achievement addiction.

Which is why personal transformation requires effort at first, but over time becomes a way of life—allowing you to stay aligned in the present while still shaping a vision for the future.

**Everything in life reflects whether you choose to grow, or remain the same.**

It's easy to believe that our wounds don't affect us as long as we don't think about them. But fragmentation doesn't disappear just because we ignore it.

You find yourself snapping at a friend, loved one, or coworker over something trivial, the heat of your reaction far outweighing the moment itself. Later, you wonder why it upset you so much, but the feeling lingers—heavy, unresolved.

You notice a pattern in your relationships: different people, same conflicts. The same wounds being reopened, the same disappointments repeating like a story you can't seem to rewrite.

You judge someone for being too much, too loud, too confident.

But deep down, is it judgment? Or is it envy?

You wonder if it's them or if—*somehow*—it's you.

Opportunities arise, doors open, but just as you step forward, something holds you back. A quiet doubt. A well-worn excuse. You convince yourself you're not ready, not worthy, not capable.

And just like that, the chance slips away—again.

Inner resistance isn't proof of failure. It's a signal that something within is ready to be liberated. When met with intention, these patterns become the very path to Inner Authority.

Misalignment leads to chronic stress, exhaustion, and emotional detachment, manifesting in our relationships, careers, self-sabotaging behaviors, and emotional activation, quietly shaping our lives from beneath the surface.

When we reject parts of ourselves, those traits don't simply go away; they turn into projections. We start seeing our unaccepted qualities reflected in others, often judging, resenting, or fixating on behaviors that secretly mirror something within us.[40]

When we are out of alignment, energy depletion accelerates and manifests as burnout. We ignore the signals inviting us to embrace the challenge, expand through it, and evolve beyond what we originally thought possible.

**When we reclaim our Inner Authority, we restore alignment and coherence across our entire system—mental, emotional, relational, and energetic.**

When we focus on developing Inner Authority, we confidently realign our lives with what replenishes us. Inner Authority requires ongoing integration and a commitment to personal reflection above external projection and fault-finding. This allows us to experience feedback not as threat or rejection but as transformational energetic information. Every activation, every tension, every conversation that doesn't sit quite right—it's all a form of feedback. And feedback, when we're ready, is a gift, revealing what's fragmented, what's coherent, and what's asking to be recalibrated.

Using that information to live in coherence, in energetic integrity with your values and purpose, and in service of the greater good is the act of alignment.

In the quantum field, the smallest changes create undeniable shifts in lived experience. By integrating quantum principles with nervous system regulation techniques, you can move from reaction to response, survival to self-leadership, dysregulation to alignment. Deep, sustainable change is not built in dramatic overhauls but through small, intentional actions repeated over time.

Inner Authority is alignment—the root of true co-creation, clear vision, an inner compass to guide the way, and confidence to act. A felt resonance between soul, strategy, and service. The voice that says, *"this is mine to do"* even when others don't see it yet.

Inner Authority, guided by Energetic Intelligence, provides the ability to tune in to the field and use that connection to examine your experiences and conditioning, in pursuit of personal alignment and in service of regenerative collective impact.

For years, I had been running from myself. From the pain I didn't have time to feel. From the parts of me shaped by survival, the painful thoughts that surfaced when I wasn't distracted. I ignored my pain through achievement—working full-time, going to school full-time, raising my daughter alone so we could both have a shot at a better life.

I hustled my way out of crisis. I didn't stop. I couldn't. And it worked—on the surface.

I made it out of my small town, into Fortune Five. I led high-impact work. I hit my professional and financial goals.

But I was leading from fragmentation—*so none of it ever felt like enough.*

My approach in those early days was driven. Sharp. Proving. Performing.

Survival strategy dressed up as confidence and masquerading as certainty.

Before I could become a conduit for healing or transformation, I had to stop outrunning myself.

Inner Authority is cultivating the capacity to integrate the past and build something new. To live in alignment, we must recognize when our ego is protecting us versus when it is limiting us.

Psychologist Alice Miller described how a lack of unconditional love can create a "false self"—a version of us built to please others. Carl Jung called this our *shadow*: the parts we repress to stay safe, accepted, or in control.[41]

Psychologist Robert A. Johnson showed that when we avoid these parts of ourselves, we often fall into patterns of self-sabotage, emotional reactivity, or unexplained resistance. Carl Jung also believed that personal transformation requires confronting the hidden aspects of our psyche: the fears, insecurities, and suppressed emotions we avoid. Johnson expanded on this, emphasizing that self-acceptance is the key to true transformation.

Ego is not the enemy. It's a protector—the *part* of us that learned to stay safe by controlling, defending, proving, or performing. In IFS terms, ego is simply a part that forms in response to fear, pain, or conditioning. It tries to keep us safe by seeking control, approval, or certainty, but it limits our growth when overactive or overutilized.

When ego is in the driver's seat, we often suppress the more vulnerable or intuitive parts of ourselves. We hide our fears, doubts, and authentic selves. This suppression forms our shadow—the hidden aspects of self that, when left unexplored, drive our behaviors from beneath the surface.

At its best, ego shields us from harm; at its worst, it keeps us stuck—seeking certainty, avoiding vulnerability, or relying on what once worked but no longer serves. When we lead from ego, we often mistake control, compliance, and submission for power.

Inner Authority, by contrast, is quiet and anchored. It doesn't defend—it discerns.

Integration is how the ego loosens its grip; recalibration restores Inner Authority. The goal is not to destroy the ego but to reconcile or reintegrate the parts of ourselves we've rejected. This means confronting painful memories *and* hidden potential.

---

**WHEN ALL PARTS OF YOU ARE ACKNOWLEDGED AND REINTEGRATED, THE EGO NO LONGER NEEDS TO GUARD, CONTROL, OR PROVE.**

---

It shifts from running the show to taking its rightful seat as one opinion among many. Helping us move beyond distortion—beyond the need to defend or be understood—and discern with intentional precision instead of reacting from fear.

**Inner Authority lives in the moments when no one else can validate your clarity but you move forward anyway.**

Much like when I had the urge to pursue a career at Amazon, after the pandemic, I felt an unmistakable nudge to move out of Supply Chain. That clarity didn't come from logic; it came from a deep internal knowing. Trusting it led to a promotion and a role better aligned with my long-term goals.

## WITH INNER AUTHORITY AND ENERGETIC INTELLIGENCE, VISION PRECEDES VALIDATION

When I felt called to speak out about leadership behaviors I believed were misaligned with psychological safety, ethical integrity, and Amazon's core principles, I knew it could cost me—professionally and relationally.

But with Inner Authority, I knew staying silent would cost more: my integrity and energetic alignment. It was uncomfortable. I was probably considered "difficult" yet again. But Inner Authority allows us to stay rooted and confident, even when others can't yet see the vision.

Inner Authority isn't always rewarded in the short term. But it always leads you back to your purpose.

Personal transformation is freeing yourself from the limitations—internal and external—that keep you from living in alignment with who you truly are. The process often follows structured psychological stages, each requiring a shift in perception, identity, and emotional maturity.[42] Early in the transformation journey, focus is primarily on understanding wounds, breaking patterns, and recognizing the ways we have been shaped by our past. Later stages require something different: integration, meaning-making, and stepping into conscious leadership—within ourselves and the world around us.

**Inner Authority and Energetic Intelligence are the gateway to Quantum Leadership.**

Energetic recalibration is the process of clearing interference and restoring internal coherence by integrating fragmented parts of the self—emotions, beliefs, and energetic patterns that were once suppressed or disowned. This allows our frequency to emerge, and from that clarity, Inner Authority is born.

In practice, energetic recalibration is about recognizing patterns, projections, and resistance, then turning inward and asking: *what is this trying to teach me about myself and my path?*

**Inner Authority is allowing your full essence to be present—without apology or restraint.**

Friction signals where unconscious patterns or fragmented parts are disrupting our energy. When we meet that friction with new awareness and different responses—again and again—we recalibrate, integrating what was once denied. This steady practice restores coherence. It aligns thought, emotion, and action and gradually expands both our frequency and influence. Alignment is sustained not just mentally or emotionally but energetically—requiring the nervous system to release old protection patterns so transformation can hold.

Integrating fragmentation goes beyond suppression or hidden emotions, digging deep into the fragmented aspects of *self* that disrupt our signal and the unconscious patterns that distort our energy until they're integrated. When we stop sending mixed signals and begin to align thought, emotion, and action our path begins to reflect that coherence. Our frequency rises and sphere of influence expands.

In alignment, choices are guided by inner truth, not by the need to prove, please, or protect. This isn't just mental, emotional, relational, or physiological—it's energetic. It is a state your entire system must sustain. If your nervous system is still patterned for protection or overactivation, it will pull you off-kilter no matter how clear your vision is.

Self-awareness and self-regulation are the foundation of Inner Authority—the ability to lead from integration rather than fragmentation. The more aligned we become, the greater our ability to shape the collective reality.

## INNER AUTHORITY IS REMEMBERING WHO YOU WERE BEFORE THE DISTORTION AND LEARNING TO LEAD FROM THAT TRUTH

Allow every part of yourself to be acknowledged, honored, and expressed. Your past does not define you, your pain is not your identity, and you are not what happened to you. You are who you choose to become.

Understanding your own fragmentation matters. This is as true in leadership as it is in our personal lives. Your nervous system shapes how you interpret signals, decide when to act, and whether you lead from authenticity or old conditioning. Coherence shapes the impact we bring to every space we enter. When we are in congruence with our character, values, and purpose, our heart rhythms synchronize with our brain waves—amplifying our ability to attract, create, and influence outcomes.

When regulated, you can respond intentionally and stay in alignment. When dysregulated, you default to reactive cycles that erode your Inner Authority—your ability to entrain, expand, and allow for emergence.

If repatterning were purely a cognitive process, integration would be easy. We would recognize our fears, acknowledge our past pain, and simply move forward. But lasting integration happens in the body. This is why recalibration requires nervous system regulation, somatic and emotional processing on a physiological level, allowing us to more accurately interpret energetics in our environments. Therapy alone is not enough if the body is still holding on to trauma. Physical health alone is not enough if the mind is consumed by stress and self-doubt.

Integration is not just about returning to a previous state. It is about becoming something new and unified. It is not about rigid discipline or pushing through at all costs. It's about balance, knowing when to lean in and when to step back.

When we begin integrating our parts, the ego's compulsion to defend or perform softens. But for many of us, that pattern of proving ourselves is deeply ingrained. From childhood, we learned that approval was safer than authenticity. Over time, early survival strategies harden into habits that keep us performing for acceptance instead of expressing our truest selves.

Integration and recalibration strengthen Inner Authority. It is all about training the brain and body to intentionally respond rather than react.

Marcus Aurelius and Seneca taught that our suffering is not caused by external events but by our interpretation of them. Epictetus emphasized radical self-control, reminding us that we cannot control what happens, but we can always control how we respond.

These perspectives are foundational to energetic recalibration, the ability to consciously process stress, challenge, and failure—and leverage that data to inform your most aligned next step.

**Recalibration + Aligned Action = Integration**

*and*

**Integration + Aligned Action = Inner Authority**

**Integration and Recalibration Equations:** Demonstrate the critical role of each in building Inner Authority through repetitive aligned action in response to challenges and expansion opportunities.

At some point in every journey, you hit a layer so deep that you hesitate before going further. The darkness is thicker here. Heavier. More resistant. It whispers to you, urging you to turn back. This is where most people stop, and the real work begins. The only way forward is to sit with it. People often speak of healing as a journey toward light—toward clarity, love, and self-acceptance. But transformation requires the courage to turn inward, to explore the hidden corners of the self, and to integrate what we've buried, denied, or feared.

I took a sabbatical to sit—*really sit*—with the pain I suppressed for years. The pain of who I had been in my worst moments. The pain of the version of me who led from fear, fury, or the ache of unworthiness. I stopped asking, "*why is this happening?*" and started asking, "*what is this feeling trying to teach me?*"

When I allowed myself to feel the things I had been avoiding, I saw them for what they really were: moments in time.

I stopped needing to prove myself and I started showing up in alignment with who I *actually* am. Not the version that fought to survive. The version that prioritizes truth, justice, and accountability in power—the version that doesn't abandon herself to meet others' expectations, or cower to make them comfortable. I reclaimed my Inner Authority as a promise to never again abandon what I know in my soul to be right.

---

**INNER AUTHORITY EMERGES AS COHERENCE STRENGTHENS, AND IT PROVIDES THE CONFIDENCE TO ACT IN ALIGNMENT WITH YOUR QUANTUM BLUEPRINT.**

---

The ability to tune in to this—for self and others—is Energetic Intelligence. Together, they form the frequency of your leadership presence and influence.

Energetic recalibration happens when you stop trying to

escape from yourself. Integration is the act of reclaiming every part of yourself—the light, the dark, and the unknown—and weaving them back into a cohesive whole. This is the difference between bypassing pain and transforming *through* it. It's how we reclaim our power, embrace our gifts, and show up as the person we *know* we were always meant to be. It is looking at the patterns that repeat in different people, different jobs, different situations, each stemming from the same core wound.

Recalibration isn't about fixing the feeling—it's about making space for it until the frequency shifts. Transformation doesn't eliminate friction, but it helps us develop the tools to navigate change and growth with self-compassion, awareness, and intention.

Transformation is simply choosing presence over protection—and meeting wounds with compassion instead of contempt. Once we learn to do this for ourselves, we can meet others with the same energy.

For me, college was about recalibration and purpose; I was rewriting my inherited destiny. As a full-time student, working and raising my daughter alone, I stayed committed to graduating because I knew education wasn't just about credentials. It was about gaining access to and successfully navigating systems that weren't intended for people like me, who started where I started. It was my way out of the cycles I had witnessed my whole life: poverty, addiction, codependency, playing small.

I was learning to think more critically, to ask better questions, to stop absorbing everything I was taught without inspection. I was building the internal infrastructure to hold a different frequency. One that didn't rely on dysfunction or overfunctioning. I didn't have the words yet for things like "Inner Authority" or "systemic misalignment," but I knew something had to change, and I was going to help do it.

Looking back, that was one of the first times I led myself solely from vision.

Inner Authority strengthens when we stop hiding, when we step fully into our light and lead from personal power. It comes from not only knowing your whole self but also recognizing and trusting the signals you receive—then choosing your response to friction with intention, integrity, and alignment.

Stepping into our light can be just as terrifying as facing our darkness. It demands that we stop making excuses, that we stop hiding—that we start living our truth, out loud.

Many of us resist our own success, our own brilliance, because we have been conditioned to believe that claiming our power is arrogant, selfish, or unsafe.

We dim ourselves to fit in, to avoid judgment, to keep the peace.

But what if the very thing you admire in someone else—their courage, their voice, their leadership, their creativity—is actually a reflection of what is waiting to be unlocked within you? What if the very thing the world needs right now is *your* unique skills, perspective, conviction, and confidence to show up?

**When we operate from Inner Authority—our presence stabilizes rather than distorts—inviting clarity, collaboration, dialogue, and growth.**

Fragmentation and misalignment keep us in survival mode, disconnected from our own wisdom *and* from each other. Without Inner Authority, we default to reacting, complying, or controlling—the very dynamics that perpetuate dysfunction in families, organizations, and systems.

Inner Authority extends our focus beyond healing and into self-actualization. It is the point when our journey shifts from integrating what felt broken to recognizing what was always whole.

You stop leading from approval, fear, or encoded patterns and start leading from coherence. You see through distortion, respond with clarity, and invite others into alignment simply by modeling integrity and courage.

When we use friction to recalibrate and take repeated aligned action, we begin integrating and closing the gap between who we are and who we say we want to be. Through repeated experience and energetic attunement, we begin to develop EnQ, which strengthens Quantum Leadership.

As the foundation to Energetic Intelligence and Quantum Leadership, Inner Authority allows us to filter through noise, transform distortion, and lead from coherence—internally and externally. Without it, distortion dominates and we default to control, reaction, and fragmentation.

Inner Authority is shaping life with intention. The more we radiate inner alignment, the more we shift the energy of every conversation, decision, and system we touch.

### BLINK

Mom gets out of rehab. We move back to the west side into a little house with her husband. It seems like a nicer area than where we've lived before. I want to have hope for this "new life," but by now I know better than to let myself get used to "good times."

Hope is a dangerous thing when survival is all you know.

One big fight and everything changes again. Just like that. Seems as if it's always that swift. And yet not swift enough.

### BLINK

Twelve. We're moving to Kettle Falls, Washington. This is where I spend the next six years of my life, from the tail end of sixth grade to high school graduation.

*I had high hopes again; usually did. Oddly optimistic. However, all my mom did was sleep. She was terribly depressed, needed to recover from decades of drug abuse, among other things. Coming back to an area that carried so much trauma of her own wouldn't work out well for any of us.*

### BLINK

What age? I don't know. My cousin comes forward about being molested by our babysitter's son.

*My memory from the sidewalk, my mom kneeling down to talk to me. It was always in the back of my mind. I wondered if that was what my memory was about.*

I ask her if I was too.

# ENERGETIC INTELLIGENCE

*"The energy of the mind is the essence of life."*
—ARISTOTLE

Energetic Intelligence—the ability to perceive, interpret, and influence the energy in self, others, and systems—is a biological and relational phenomenon that determines which signals we transmit—fear or safety, control or trust, suppression or expansion. This becomes the underlying *operating system* for maintaining coherence and inviting continued expansion.

**Energetic Intelligence is how we receive and respond to subtle cues from the quantum field. It's the bridge between internal coherence and external action.**

When we return to coherence, we become open channels for Quantum Intelligence to move through, guiding our choices with greater ease and reliability. When coherence expands into the field of possibility, we embody Quantum Leadership—where intention, energy, and interconnectedness influence interactions and shape outcomes in real time.

As we shift internally, the systems we lead begin to respond and reorganize as well.

It is more than mental conviction—it's a full-body knowing anchored in energetic integrity. When we regulate our emotions, tune in to the body's signals, and allow space for presence, we create the conditions for Quantum Intelligence to communicate directly. Clarity replaces noise, recalibration replaces reaction, and personal transformation becomes tangible.

## QUANTUM INTELLIGENCE IS THE FIELD WE TUNE IN TO—ENERGETIC INTELLIGENCE IS HOW

Unlike traditional models that center on awareness or regulation alone, Quantum Leadership and EnQ emphasize adaptive application—how leaders use energetic data to make decisions, dissolve resistance, and facilitate systemic coherence.

Energy moves through our nervous system, fascia, and electromagnetic field—shaping our thoughts, emotions, and experiences. When these systems are balanced, we experience clarity, alignment, and stability. When they are overactive or underactive, we experience emotional imbalances, health issues, and inner turmoil.

Energetic Intelligence is your ability to notice subtle cues—deeper breathing, tension behind words, a shift in tone—and respond in ways that restore or maintain *your* coherence before responding to the external environment.

It is the ability to *attune* to the energy of the field and your internal signal in real time. Cultivating EnQ turns transformation into a daily practice of experiencing, interpreting, and managing personal energetics (thought, emotion, intention, integrity).

As a component of Quantum Leadership, EnQ connects personal transcendence with collective transformation by treating energy not just as a state to manage but as a strategic medium through which influence is *exercised* and change is *channeled*.

Quantum principles remind us that energy precedes matter, observation collapses potential into form, and conscious choice in these moments—the zero point—is where potential becomes reality.

As energy interacts, friction emerges, inviting us back into conscious choice. Each micro decision creates a new reality, a different outcome, amplifying coherence or fragmentation.

To ground this concept further, it's helpful to review the primary intelligences that govern human behavior and leadership presence.

| | Intelligence | Focus | Key Competencies | Leadership Application |
|---|---|---|---|---|
| **Head** | IQ (Cognitive) | Logic, analysis, execution. | Strategic thinking, problem-solving, focus. | Making decisions, managing complexity, systems planning. |
| **Heart** | EQ (Emotional) | Emotions and relationships. | Emotional regulation, empathy, communication. | Navigating conflict, motivating teams, relational repair. |
| **Horizon** | YQ (Inquiry) | Expansion, possibility, and awareness. | Meta-cognition, pattern recognition, meaning-making. | Visionary, adaptive, systems focus; navigating ambiguity. |
| **Field** | EnQ (Energetic) | Subtle energy and frequency. | Attunement, discernment, coherence; pattern anticipation. | Shifting culture, leading by presence, field impact; foresight. |
| **Faith** | SQ (Spiritual) | Meaning, values, purpose. | Moral reasoning, integrity, visionary clarity. | Resilient leadership, principled decision-making, shapes legacy. |

**Intelligences that Shape Human and Leadership Potential:** These five intelligences shape how we think, feel, and lead. Each governs a distinct aspect of awareness and behavior.

As you may already know, Intellectual Intelligence (IQ) is how we process information, solve problems, and make decisions. Emotional Intelligence (EQ) helps us navigate our feelings and relationships. Spiritual Intelligence (SQ) connects us to a greater sense of meaning and values.

While IQ, EQ, and SQ are increasingly understood in psychology and leadership theory, Quantum Leadership regularly harnesses two additional types: Inquiry Quotient (YQ) and Energetic Intelligence (EnQ).

Inquiry Quotient (YQ), the disciplined curiosity that challenges assumptions and reframes possibilities, is a core skill that underlies all transformation and Quantum Strategy—asking better questions, expanding perspective, and unlocking new possibilities.[43] Energetic Intelligence (EnQ) is understanding and navigating the subtle field of energy that informs our presence, decisions, and influence.

IQ shapes how we think and solve problems, EQ guides how we connect, SQ anchors us to meaning, YQ encourages us to expand, and EnQ reveals, regulates, and influences the energetic field underpinning it all. EnQ transcends what we feel, believe, or interpret in the subtle frequencies behind our thoughts, feelings, actions, and interactions—to include how that energy influences our environment in any given moment.

You don't need to exemplify all of these to be a great leader, but recognizing which you naturally default to, prefer, or are gifted in—*and* appreciating the same in others—helps you interpret and influence the energy in the room, shape culture, and guide outcomes by first managing your own energetic signature.

EQ strengthens awareness and regulation of your inner world. EnQ builds on this—attuning to the energetic field between people, the environment, and the unspoken influences shaping connection, trust, and impact.

---

**WHEN THESE INTELLIGENCES WORK IN HARMONY, LEADERSHIP TRANSCENDS INFLUENCE TO BECOME A CATALYST FOR TRANSFORMING PEOPLE AND SYSTEMS.**

---

Energetic Intelligence explains the difference between a tense room that shuts down ideas and a relaxed one where people are comfortable asking, *"what if?"*

Subtle shifts in your tone or focus can tip the energy in one direction or the other. Imagine walking into a meeting where everyone's guarded versus one where the leader's calm confidence makes collaboration feel easy—same team, different field, different results.

**EnQ is how coherence becomes clarity and presence becomes power.**

For years, I thought transformation was purely about mindsets and belief systems. If I could just think my way into alignment, everything would fall into place. But thought alone doesn't create coherence; it requires embodied energetic alignment.

Emotional Intelligence research shows that emotional regulation and self-awareness are key to managing energy levels. People who master their internal states conserve energy, while those who react impulsively experience rapid depletion.[44]

Every emotion carries an energetic signature—one that either expands or contracts your ability to create, connect, and lead. EnQ operates at the quantum level—sensing resonance, receptivity, and systemic coherence in real time. Unlike personality or intent, which reflect patterns and desires, EnQ tracks a person's energetic state in the moment, including our own—inviting us to observe alignment and integrity as a dynamic signal in real time.

The difference between reparative recalibration and further destruction lies in whether we approach misalignment early with openness and co-creation, or allow it to calcify into dysfunction and burnout. Fragmentation and misalignment make increased friction and burnout more likely. EnQ can detect these issues before they become bigger. Reparative recalibration increases awareness, personal accountability, expansive dialogue, and the development of a shared vision.

## MISALIGNMENT LEADS TO BURNOUT—INNER AUTHORITY AND ENERGETIC INTELLIGENCE ARE THE ANTIDOTES

Energetic Intelligence carries you when you don't have the answers and the path is unclear.

One of the reasons energetic misalignment is so difficult to address is that it can stem from vastly different origins: trauma, social conditioning, personality, or systemic oppression—and often, a mix of all four. From the outside, resulting behaviors may look similar: reactivity, defensiveness, resistance to feedback, or performance-driven distortion. But what they need in response varies greatly. Trauma needs attunement. Conditioning needs unlearning. Personality needs integration.

Energetic Intelligence doesn't claim to diagnose root causes; it is a tool for navigating the signal—for evaluating what's present and discerning how (or whether) to engage. The Quantum Leadership Quadrant doesn't assign people static labels; it provides a dynamic map for identifying the relational terrain and adjusting accordingly, with as much compassion as clarity.

Energy is something you can *feel*. Some days, everything flows: your mind is clear, your body is relaxed, and small tasks feel effortless. Other days, everything feels heavy, slow, or jagged. That's misalignment. These fluctuations aren't mood swings; they're signals from your body and the field, showing us where energy is stuck or scattered—asking to be regulated, restored, and recalibrated.

Energy is data—entering your field of awareness for a reason.

**The more attuned you are to those frequencies, the faster you can interpret the quantum signals embedded in your reactions, behaviors, and desires—as well as those of others.**

Energetic Intelligence restores integration across brain states. When we regulate and align, the prefrontal cortex comes back online, reconnecting us to foresight, creativity, and ethical reasoning. The nervous system shifts out of hypervigilance, opening space for safety and connection. Reward and empathy circuits rebalance so our drive for achievement aligns with meaning, trust, and long-term impact rather than short-term gain. On a collective level, coherence is contagious. Mirror neurons and social entrainment create shared rhythms that amplify collaboration and possibility. EnQ transforms the fragmented spiral of survival and self-interest into an opportunity for expansive growth toward integrity, connection, and collective progress.

EQ helps you manage your emotions. EnQ helps you tune into energy—yours, others', and the collective field, leveraging it as data and insight. SQ connects us to Quantum Intelligence. It deepens our sense of meaning and purpose, connecting us to conscious awareness and ethical wisdom. EQ helps you not cause harm, EnQ helps you amplify good.

Energetic Intelligence isn't conceptual—it's experiential. For many, the entry point is a moment of embodied awareness in the present moment.

In 2018, I started meditating obsessively. Hours a day, visualizing my energy centers spinning, focusing on clearing blockages and practicing intentional release. I always felt this current running through me; now I was learning how to work with it intentionally.

At first, it was just about survival, as were most things then. I needed to feel different, lighter, more at peace. As I deepened my practice, things began to shift. Vivid dreams. Unexplained vertigo. An intense *pop* right between my eyes during one meditation. I could feel energy moving through my body with specificity. Electronics would glitch or completely crash when I entered a room. Thoughts and insights would arrive unprompted, bypassing logic, and later prove to be true.

Energy plays a role in how we experience life. Consciously rewiring the nervous system strengthens cognitive flexibility, creating new immediate responses that help us move from fragmented effort to coherent, aligned action—the gateway to quantum leaps.

Energy itself is a finite resource. If we don't manage it intentionally, we burn out, not just physically but mentally and emotionally as well. Burnout is prolonged energetic incoherence—and it happens when we override internal misalignment for too long. When we pour energy into people, places, and systems that don't align with our character, values, and purpose, our nervous system stays in overdrive, coherence breaks down, and energy leaks out faster than it can be restored.

I used to think discipline was the key to success. I believed that if I just worked harder, if I just pushed through exhaustion, I would get to where I wanted to be. But discipline without alignment is just self-inflicted punishment.

I've used Energetic Intelligence for as long as I can remember. As a child, it was my survival skill—reading the subtle shifts in tone, body language, and atmosphere in rooms filled with addicts and unpredictable people—a quiet certainty before logic caught up.

I learned to sense both danger and opportunity before they became visible, which later guided life-altering choices like knowing when to leave my job at System for a shot at an explosive career with Amazon, recognizing when to exit roles before dynamics turned toxic, and even anticipating head count cuts before they were announced. Over and over, Energetic Intelligence has steered me—from logic and a clear inner signal I could hear and feel before I could explain.

As I was developing this skill professionally, a new policy was being introduced and landing poorly during an all-team meeting. The room grew tense. People shifted in their seats, brows furrowed, the energy thick with unspoken concern. My senior manager began to falter, her voice tightening as questions turned pointed. I caught her glance, wide-eyed and uncertain, asking for help. I was leading the initiative, so I stepped in and acknowledged the concerns, assuring the group that while the policy was in motion, we were seeking feedback and willing to adapt. The mood shifted immediately. People softened. The conversation became collaborative instead of confrontational.

During one of the most intense projects of my career—in supply chain during the pandemic—my director was championing my L7 promotion, but I could feel their political capital eroding with their peers. Energetically, I knew my path forward in that role was closing. Instead of pushing harder, I prioritized my health and stepped back. My intuition was right—they left the company shortly after I went on sabbatical. When I returned, I stepped into a role that was truly aligned and appropriately scoped.

Another time, in a strategic-planning event, the director's breakout instructions skipped a critical element—resourcing and capacity, something every leader must weigh. I asked a clarifying question to bring that into the conversation.

Her reaction felt tense, so I grounded myself.

I had a choice: react defensively, or stay grounded, co-creative, and intentional. Anchoring into my seat, I felt the weight of my legs, the soles of my feet pressing into the floor, and I softened my face.

From that energy, I clarified that my point was for us—L7 leaders—to ensure breakout teams factored in resources and capacity before committing to a plan. Her posture softened. She smiled and agreed. A few peers later thanked me for voicing what they were thinking.

I stayed in my energy, held my standards, and modeled the very presence I believe leaders must cultivate. By maintaining my own energetic integrity, I could still serve the room, even if it made someone within it uncomfortable.

Energetic Intelligence is knowing when to observe, move, speak—and how to hold your energetic sovereignty—so your presence shifts the field toward mutual accountability and expansion without collapsing into people-pleasing or escalating tension.

**Energetic Intelligence is a skill anyone can cultivate.**

It is learning to decipher between ego and Quantum Intelligence and listening to your guidance system to discover how you receive and interpret subtle energy. For me, I get a subtle nudge in the same spot every time I receive important insight.

For years, I chased that L7 promotion at Amazon. I worked

for it, more than earned it, and yet every time I got close, the door slammed shut. I tried to prove myself more, but no matter what I did, the resistance only grew. I was drained in a way that no amount of effort could fix. I convinced myself that pushing harder was the solution, that if I just kept *striving*, I'd finally reach the level of success that would make it all worth it.

But my inner guidance knew the truth before my mind caught up. EnQ always does. I was never being blocked; I was being redirected. The moment I let go—truly surrendered—my energy returned, the path opened up, and the promotion followed quicky.

Activating EnQ means shifting from reacting to consciously creating—learning to approach life from the present moment more than the past or the future, and to continuously identify and decipher new data as it arises.

**Energetic Intelligence and Inner Authority do not come from control but from learning how to stay present in discomfort.**

While Quantum Intelligence is the field itself—an infinite, ever-present consciousness we co-create with—it is also continually influenced by others. Energetic Intelligence is the ability to attune to the field and co-create through conscious alignment, not force or control. EnQ is our capacity to sense and shift energy.

In OTS, one director's abrupt decision to end collaboration taught me the difference between structural control and energetic expansion. In FBA, the dynamic of my leaders—steeped in silence, triangulation, and institutional misalignment, including those who slyly attempted to take credit for my work—revealed what happens when positional power replaces integrity and when energetic misalignment masquerades as success.

Each experience offered the opportunity to clarify my values, character, and purpose. Each helped me remember how to trust my Energetic Intelligence and Inner Authority—how to stand in my power and confidently challenge existing systems.

In UV, I learned how subtle misalignments can rapidly derail trust and efficacy, while CommOps taught me that even people who know better will misuse the system for their own benefit, creating unhealthy environments that project the illusion of progress while eroding collaboration, innovation, and psychological safety.

At the time, these felt like rejections and barriers. Now I see them as data points—initiations into a deeper form of leadership that ultimately guided me home to myself and my unique blueprint.

When a five-day return-to-office mandate was enacted, I called it what it was: a blanket policy that ignored context and culture. Someone half-jokingly said, "*we can't say that.*" But my response was simple: that's exactly what leaders should do. Every day, we are responsible for asking whether those in charge are upholding the mission, vision, and values we agreed to—and if not, to model and demand better.

**Energetic Intelligence is the ability to consciously influence your reality by becoming the most coherent version of yourself.**

Society conditions us to suppress this innate awareness, but we can reclaim it. For years, I dismissed these experiences as coincidence. But the signs were always there. Synchronicities, gut instincts, recurring symbols. Numbers appearing at just the right time. Conversations that felt like coded messages.

When I was in high school, I read *The Secret of the Ages* by Robert Collier. From then on, I committed to decoding life's messages—using intuition and divine guidance to shape my reality. "Manifestation" wasn't just a practice; it became my way of navigating the world. Over time, I realized what I was actually learning to do was manage my own frequency—how to read, regulate, and refine my inner state to create alignment between intention and outcome.

## THE QUANTUM FIELD ISN'T JUST OBSERVING AND BEING OBSERVED—IT IS CONSTANTLY COMMUNICATING AND CO-CREATING

Energetic Intelligence begins within, but once embodied, it becomes a frequency that others can feel. Inner coherence creates a state of entrainment, where your internal rhythms synchronize with the energetic patterns of your environment. In this state, you're not forcing alignment; you're inviting resonance, allowing your field to amplify influence and sustain transformation effortlessly. This coherence enables co-creation—serving your sphere in the ways only you can, and influencing outcomes by collaborating with life itself to shape a reality that reflects personal integrity and collective possibility.

**Coherence is catalytic—personally and systemically.**

As chief of staff, I warned my L8 peers about the likelihood of requisition and hiring delays during a layoff period, only to be dismissed. "I think it'll be a bright light," they said.

We were ultimately delayed more than three months.

In another instance, following an OP1 review, the VP asked for a follow-up with the director. The director's Biz Ops partner heard differently and scheduled a follow-up with the whole team. I knew the meeting was for the director only, and that we would be asked to reduce headcount and funding requests—to do more with less.

When Andy Jassy, president and CEO of Amazon, later signaled that exact shift in his 2024 shareholder letter prioritizing leaner management, I didn't want or need it, but my EnQ felt validated. It was like the field whispered, *"you're tuned in, you knew."*

Energetic Intelligence is the resolve that guides you to move forward—despite chaos or uncertainty—anchored in the ability to attune to seen and unseen forces, to return to coherence, and expand through challenges.

EnQ complements other intelligences but depends on balanced inquiry, alignment, and integration; otherwise, access becomes distorted or inconsistent. Inner Authority provides the compass; EnQ provides the signal.

Together, they form the foundation of Quantum Leadership—enabling leaders to sense, align with, and operate from coherence in real time. The practice strengthens as we learn to leverage each intelligence as needed, flowing with circumstance while maintaining personal sovereignty and alignment. When emotional, spiritual, and cognitive intelligence align with our intentions, our physiology, presence, and actions enter a state of resonance—amplifying clarity, intuition, and magnetism.[45]

When you are deeply, personally attuned, you lead differently. You stop grasping and start guiding, and your very presence begins to shift what's possible for everyone around you, or in your sphere of influence.

**Quantum Leaders don't wait for permission or external validation; they become the embodiment of their vision *now*.**

They trust in the unseen before it materializes. They move with intention, knowing that their internal state directly influences external outcomes. They don't force outcomes; they align with them. They don't chase external success; they become the energetic match for what they seek to create. This is the shift—from chasing power to embodying it, from reacting to leading, from waiting to intentionally co-creating.

When Inner Authority meets embodied frequency, we no longer seek power outside ourselves—we become it.

We no longer strive to control outcomes. We attune to those that are aligned. We become both the tuning fork and the field it resonates within, able to meet life's complexity with responsiveness and grace.

Fragmentation may appear similar across individuals, but its origins vary. Whether rooted in trauma, personality, or conditioning, EnQ does not seek to diagnose *why* fragmentation exists but offers a compassionate tool for navigating it. This is especially relevant in environments where coherence is misread and coherent leaders are misperceived—as their presence agitates misalignment in others.

Energetic Intelligence requires tuning in to, regulating, and aligning *your* energy so you can discern what's yours and what belongs to the environment. Without this grounding, we risk projecting our own state onto others or misreading the field entirely. When you've mastered EnQ for yourself, you can approach the energy of others with clarity, neutrality, and integrity.

**The *Quantum Blueprint* is a call to stop outsourcing your power, remember who you are, live your purpose and lead by example— starting with your energy.**

## BLINK

Fifteen. New Year's Eve, loud music, people crammed around the kitchen island. I've just done my first flaming Dr. Pepper with my mom, her boyfriend, and my little brother.

Room spinning. Laughter too loud. Pretending I'm fine. My mom hands me another.

## BLINK

My resentment for her grows with each day. One day, we get into a fist fight. My mom tells my Grandma Doll about it, and she calls CPS. They come to ask me about it, at school of all places. I tell them nothing happened.

*My mom had CPS called on her a lot. She trained us at an early age not to say anything. By then, she didn't have to remind me of the expectation. Shortly after that, she decided to move back to Spokane, giving me the option to stay or go.*

So I moved in with my Grandma. By then, I was basically living as an emancipated minor. For the first time in my life, I could breathe. Her stability gave me space to finally be a kid—which, at that time, meant weekend bonfires and cheap beer. She had rules, but she also knew she couldn't control me. I craved independence, and she let me have it, while still giving me a safe space to return to every day. I knew graduation was only two years away, and then I'd be on my own again, but for a brief window I had room to explore myself without the constant weight of survival.

*My friends used to say I was so lucky my mom let me do what I wanted. To me, it just felt like she didn't care. I wanted so badly for her to care—for someone to care enough to say no.*

## BLINK

By seventeen, I'm repeating cycles I grew up in: alcohol, drugs, promiscuity, abusive relationships. Drinking most weekends eventually turns into cocaine during the week—until it finally catches up with me.

*When Coach kicked me off the basketball team, I could see in his eyes how difficult it was for him. He cared.*

## BLINK

Someone from work invites me to a party. Music, beer, the usual. A few people leave to go on a beer run. A few of us stay to play a game. A hallway. A bedroom. Two hold me down, and one climbs on top.

*He held me down and looked me in the eyes, wiping my tears as his friend raped me.*

# NAVIGATE

>>>>>>>>

USE MULTIPLE DATA SOURCES TO PROGRESS TOWARD GOALS, GROWTH, AND SYSTEMIC EVOLUTION

# 9

# INTERPERSONAL ENERGETICS

> *"The most important thing in communication is hearing what isn't said."*
> —PETER DRUCKER

Energetic Intelligence isn't just a personal practice—it's relational. We cultivate it through reflection, repair, and resonance with others. But it begins and ends *within*. When we meet our own fragmentation with compassion, we gain the capacity to witness others' with the same—and that is a bridge to our own transformation.

Relationships are where our fragmented parts get activated the most, where we see our unconscious wounds reflected back to us.

In the context of EnQ and Quantum Leadership, relationships amplify our internal world.

**Transformation is not a solitary journey. It is a cycle, moving between self-exploration and relational reflection, between solitude and integration.**

Self-actualization is refined through relationships, reflection, and a willingness to confront the unconscious parts of ourselves. It is an ongoing journey of integrating new awareness with aligned action, energy work, and conscious co-creation—continually unfolding into the next vision, the next version of ourselves, the next step in becoming.

Human connection is a critical part of nervous system regulation. Co-regulation—the ability of one person's regulated nervous system to influence another's—is an act of entrainment. Our systems begin to sync, not just emotionally but energetically, creating the conditions for mutual healing and transformation.

Healthy co-regulation and entrainment support autonomy and alignment, but tip into codependency when one person sacrifices personal authority to maintain another's regulation or harmony. Codependency can also appear in leadership when we rely on others to simply follow instructions instead of inviting dialogue and co-creation—confusing compliance with agreement. Approached intentionally, relational EnQ strengthens both coherence and autonomy, so growth emerges without collapse into dependency.

When we learn to navigate relational conflict with self-awareness, regulation, and accountability, we embody the frequency that powers Quantum Leadership.

Leadership lives everywhere—in how we navigate corporate settings, and yes, in our relationships.

Research in relationship psychology—from Imago Relationship Therapy to John Gottman's decades of work on couples—shows that we often seek relationships that mirror our unresolved wounds, offering opportunities for recalibration, repair, and reconnection.[46] When viewed through the lens of Quantum Intelligence, this research affirms that the energy we bring to relationships, consciously or subconsciously, influences their outcomes.

Much of what we label as conflict is simply the collision of different intelligences—one person leading from analysis, another from intuition, another from relational attunement. When we mistake these differences for opposition, we fragment. But when we learn to recognize and value each, conflict becomes creative tension: the raw material for innovative solutions. Quantum Leaders cultivate the field to hold a diversity of strengths, and guide their integration into outcomes no single perspective could have achieved alone.

The moment I recognized that my relationships were reflecting my own wounds back to me, I stopped blaming and started tuning in. I looked at my marriage, past relationships, my friendships, dynamics with coworkers, and even my interactions with random people who activated something in me, and I started seeing it as feedback on where I needed to grow.

The times I felt abandoned? An illumination of the parts of myself I had abandoned.

The people who triggered anger or frustration? Projections of disowned parts of myself.

---

**INTERPERSONAL ENERGETICS GOES BEYOND HOW WE RELATE TO OTHERS—THE DEEPER POWER LIES IN USING IT TO EXPERIENCE, INTERPRET, AND MANAGE OUR OWN ENERGY IN THE PRESENCE OF OTHERS.**

---

Transformation wasn't about who surrounded me—it came from becoming the most whole, healed version of myself while navigating relational friction. While our original interpersonal patterns are shaped from our earliest moments (family dynamics, social norms, gender expectations), once imprinted, the way we navigate new experiences either reinforces old wounds or turns those early moments into material for personal transformation, integration, and energetic recalibration.

I've come to understand relationships as one of the greatest tools for reflection and conscious evolution beyond inherited and learned patterns. But without this awareness, I didn't know how to recognize these reflections for what they were at the time, often leading to greater suffering, disconnection, and delayed progress.

When we attune to Inner Authority and embody wholeness, we naturally bring coherence into every interaction. In this state, our presence communicates steadiness and clarity, inviting trust and easing defensiveness. This strengthens relationships and influences the collective field of leadership, where coherence becomes contagious and new possibilities emerge.

When we choose alignment, we stabilize our own field. In that stability, others can more easily attune to their truth. Personal alignment is a contribution to the collective consciousness; each act of transformation sends a signal that invites others into coherence.

Despite our interconnected reality, modern society conditions us to believe in separateness. We are taught that we must compete for success. That our struggles are ours to carry alone. That we are isolated, individual beings moving through a chaotic world.

Interconnectedness means seeing ourselves in another, recognizing the same universal longing for understanding, acceptance, and peace. When we integrate this truth, love ceases to be conditional or transactional. It becomes a state of being, an ever-expanding force that extends beyond personal relationships and into the collective.

You've likely felt this before in social movements, at concerts, in moments of collective silence or celebration, or in the energetic shift that occurs when organizational or political leadership changes.

To understand how we relate, we explore what we've been taught to suppress, perform, or deny. From early childhood, societal norms and gender expectations begin shaping our sense of self, influencing what emotions are safe to express, what roles we're expected to play, and how we seek or suppress connection. These patterns become the energetic imprint we unconsciously carry into adult relationships, leadership, and identity.

**By bringing awareness to these imprints, we gain the power to choose coherence over conditioning—and to co-create from our deepest alignment and integrity.**

Transformation (or lack thereof) doesn't just impact you; it affects your relationships, communities, and the systems of power you exist within. When we fail to integrate our own fragmentation, it shows up in how we treat others, in our relational patterns, in the way we engage with the world.

Prior to Amazon, I once had a leader tell me I needed to be okay with my direct reports calling me "baby" if I wanted to work in the field I was in. That's not resilience. That's resignation. An example of distorted leadership rooted in unresolved fragmentation, where fear is passed off as wisdom and trauma is mistaken for tradition.

When we stop seeing relationships as sources of pain and start recognizing them as portals for transformation—ours and others'—we reclaim power over our circumstances. Every misunderstanding, every moment of connection or dissonance carries wisdom—providing the opportunity to practice deciphering self versus others and self versus the environment.

Instead of "What is their problem?" we begin to ask, "What is this revealing about me?" In doing so, we free ourselves from cycles of blame and victimhood and step into deeper responsibility for our own energy and the reality we co-create.

**Every connection serves a purpose, even when it brings challenges and discomfort.**

Relationships are where we learn to sense energy, respond instead of react, and embody alignment in real time. We repeat experiences to release karma and to recalibrate energy. The most important relationships—the ones that challenge us, expand us, and demand our growth—are not about creating comfort; they are about creating space.

Space to evolve, to heal, to confront the parts of ourselves that we would otherwise avoid.

My early experiences taught me that love was conditional, that relationships required constant hypervigilance, and that my needs were secondary to maintaining peace. This created an unconscious template of avoidance and hyper-independence, where I struggled to fully receive love or let others in.

But attachment isn't destiny. Research suggests that attachment styles are fluid. They can evolve with self-awareness, healing, and intentional shifts in behavior. This means we aren't trapped in the relational patterns we inherited; we can rewrite them. In doing so, we can alter the way we relate and make decisions, both at home and in the workplace.

## QUANTUM LEADERSHIP IS DETERMINED BY THE COHERENCE YOU HOLD OR THE CHAOS YOU PASS ON

When I was responsible for transforming the continuous improvement culture across a nearly six-thousand-person organization, I started by assessing the current landscape with several key leaders. Then, I shared my vision and proposal for uniting siloed excellence teams into a centralized team and function—with three distinct implementation paths to pick from.

I wanted to honor local nuance, maintain regionally dispersed sub-teams, train existing IT talent rather than build a team of specialists, and center shared vision over redundant hierarchy to scale impact.

I knew from experience that most cultural transformations of this scale take three to five years. I aimed to shift it in eighteen months or less. I'd done it before—twice—but in organizations one-tenth the size.

The challenge and the possibilities inspired me.

It was the epitome of being an Amazonian—seeing an opportunity, moving quickly to address it, and driving alignment to accelerate progress.

I built traction with the people most affected and those closest to the work. But then a newly hired director entered the scene. As mentioned earlier, in our first meeting he immediately squashed the idea.

There was little curiosity about the alignment already underway, and momentum stalled under a more authoritative, command-first approach.

Having to backtrack and gain buy-in from new leaders was nothing new—leaders come and go frequently. So, despite his initial hesitation, I advanced the proposal through an additional review, navigating subtle politics and overt resistance.

I sought support, and I was told, "I can't tell him what to do."

That's not what I was asking for, but it *was* peak irony. These same people had no problem telling *me* what to do.

*Why?*

In that moment, any remaining attachment to being seen as agreeable or deferential dissolved.

Again and again, I found myself in rooms where I could read the energetic dynamics before they caught up. I could feel it again. The leadership I encountered leaned laissez-faire, risk-averse under pressure, quietly protective of established practice. My perspective wasn't inconvenient because it lacked merit. It was inconvenient because it challenged a system built to reward comfort and the status quo.

My mission was clear: I wasn't just shifting the process improvement culture; I was shaking up underlying power structures. At the time, I was still learning to trust what I sensed before I had hard evidence. The behaviors themselves weren't new in leadership culture, but recognizing them early and choosing to act from coherence instead of compliance? That was new for *me*.

Over the next six months, I ran the annual strategic planning process for the entire organization and secured a 250 percent increase for my team, amid a historic round of layoffs at Amazon—a major vote of confidence from my finance and leadership team—and a signal that I knew what I was doing, and they did too.

As layoffs arrived, inner distortion and dysregulation within the leadership team amplified due to increased stress; friction and microaggressions also intensified.

I was repeatedly left out of meetings for initiatives I had previously been part of, excluded from critical talent discussions despite being the only woman in the room, and told my perspective "wouldn't have made a difference" in key layoff communication decisions.

At the beginning of the next year, the same director who stifled the IT transformation asked to meet with me to "offer suggestions" on how I could better serve his team. By this point, his leadership pattern was clear to me; invitations to "collaborate" were less about open dialogue and more about securing agreement with a predetermined course of action.

I knew the conversation wasn't about exploring possibilities—it was about reasserting control.

When I didn't immediately agree to scrap my plans and cater to his sudden, misplaced urgency, he doubled down—insisting on explaining again what he thought I should do and how I should do it.

I listened, paused, then replied: "I hear what you're saying. I just don't agree with you."

He froze. Then closed his laptop, abruptly ended the conversation, and walked out—confirming for me that he was not interested in my ideas or having an open dialogue.

He sought my compliance and didn't know how to handle my refusal to provide it.

I didn't need or want his approval. I had already done the energetic, strategic, and personal work to trust the signals and stand firm in my alignment—confidently pressing against the comfort zones of those who, knowingly or not, upheld systems of harm, dysfunction, and subjugation.

The old me would have internalized the rejection and looked for ways to smooth things over, to appease. This version of me let the rejection reveal the truth of the system, and in doing so, I didn't just reclaim my own authority. I modeled what it means to stay rooted so that those who came after me might inherit something other than exclusion disguised as ignorance or indifference.

**Internal and interpersonal friction, when navigated energetically with intention, leads to deeper Inner Authority, power, and purpose.**

Reflecting on early parts of my career, I was used to tackling work others didn't want to navigate—or didn't want to own. As a deeply action-oriented person with relentlessly high standards, I often became the go-to for turnaround initiatives, team restructuring, and high-profile or rapid transformations. Role after role, within three months or less, I recovered roadmaps, immediately improved efficiency, and led my own separate passion projects.

In one instance, it became clear that I was being used to remove evidence of other people's ineffective leadership. I'd get tapped; results would immediately follow. Yet I wasn't being supported in the growth I'd asked for. The more I succeeded, the more I felt people around me wanted to contain, ignore, or devalue my presence. In another instance I mentioned earlier, while attempting to discuss the systemic elements of Amazon's impact in local communities—a key part of my role at the time—conviction was mistaken for challenge, strategic recommendations were dismissed as mere philosophy, and my questions triggered contempt in a leader who hadn't done their own self-inquiry.

The moments that activate something inside us are most often the ones that hold the lesson we need in that moment. You can take things at surface level, react to what someone says or does, and insist they fit into your box, or you can pause and ask: *what is this inviting me to inspect and explore?*

The value of Inner Authority and Energetic Intelligence shines in how we navigate resistance and relationships—reminding us that we are not responsible for other people's energy, only for how we show up.

We have a responsibility to say something when we see harm, but we also have a responsibility to let people make their own mistakes. The work of discernment is knowing where one ends and the other begins.

**Their reactions weren't about me. They were about the way I made them feel about themselves.**

When people lead from fear, conviction will always feel like a threat.

When I zoomed out—team after team—I realized it wasn't a *me* problem. Their responses were a feature in a system designed to reward output at the expense of humanity. A system that talks about psychological safety while pushing performative belonging. A system that's so used to control-based management that it hasn't paused to recognize Energetic Intelligence and Quantum Leadership as an advantage for people and performance.

**Interpersonal Energetics is a critical foundation of Quantum Leadership, relational evolution, and collective transformation.**

Every interaction transmits energy—consciously or not. When our motivation stems from self-preservation or personal gain over collective alignment, it's *felt*. This dynamic often shows up in toxic teams, exclusionary cultures, or leadership blind spots.

When we embrace relationships as sacred opportunities for expansion, we stop running from the lessons they bring. We soften, we grow, and we expand together.

Some wounds won't be verbally resolved or emotionally validated. But that doesn't mean they need to stay active in our field. In these cases, forgiveness is an energetic act—releasing and recalibrating.

This doesn't excuse what happened, but it does release the energetic tether it holds over us.

Forgiveness is not just about healing relationships with others; it is about healing the relationship we have with ourselves, with our past, and with the greater unfolding of our soul's purpose. It's about trusting that even painful moments are woven into a greater divine choreography.

Our interpersonal field is shaped by the energy we carry, the wounds we've integrated, and the patterns we're willing to challenge. When we carry resentment, we remain energetically bonded to the wound and the version of ourselves shaped by it. Compassion, then, becomes a form of surrender—a conscious choice to no longer fuel that loop with our life force.

Instead of asking *why did this happen to me*, we begin to ask, *what is this here to teach me?*

As we transform internally, the energetic quality of our relationships transforms too. What we perceive, how we relate, and how others experience us is deeply shaped by the relationship we hold with ourselves. The way we communicate, set boundaries, and lead becomes a living reflection of our evolution and alignment.

**Relationships are shaped by self-awareness, perception, and communication.**

The way we see ourselves, the way others perceive us, and the unspoken dynamics that exist between people shape the depth and success of any team, community, and organization—influencing how trust is built, boundaries are honored, and mutual growth is sustained.

The Johari Window provides a valuable framework for understanding how perception influences relationships—both personal and professional.[47] Developed by Joseph Luft and Harrington Ingham, the model reveals that we all have aspects of ourselves that are known to us, blind spots that others see but we do not, hidden aspects we choose not to share, and unknown elements waiting to be discovered. Charles Handy later applied this model to leadership, showing that reducing blind spots and hidden areas leads to deeper trust, collaboration, and more effective relationships.[48]

Building on this and the Quantum Leadership Quadrant, Johari 2.0 adds another lens by layering self-awareness, openness to feedback, and integration capacity into the energetic architecture of leadership. Our character, values, and purpose form the foundation of alignment, and when lived in service, they create coherence others can trust.

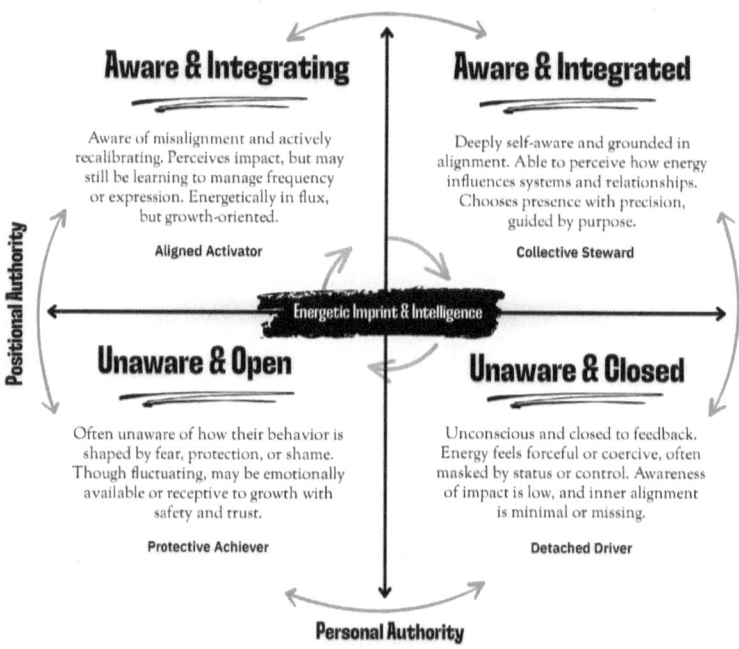

**Johari 2.0:** An evolution of the original Johari Window, this model expands awareness beyond perception into energy and influence—illustrating how self-knowledge, environmental data, and presence interact—revealing not only what is seen or unseen, but how energy shapes connection, trust, and impact, especially during conflict.

While the Quantum Leadership Quadrant maps the Energetic Frequency and Intelligence leaders carry into a room, along with the authority source they lean on, this Johari-inspired lens reveals whether a leader is willing to explore opportunities and navigate friction—while we focus on maintaining our own energetic steadiness, frequency, and integrity.

The traditional Johari Window helps us understand how perception shapes relationships and leadership through hidden and unknown areas. Energetic Intelligence allows us to sense the base frequency in a room or relationship—whether it feels protective, open, or something in between. What we perceive may differ from what others experience, shaped by interpersonal dynamics and our own levels of awareness and integration across EQ, SQ, and EnQ.

For example, a Protective Achiever and a Detached Driver may both hold positional authority, but the former operates from guarded self-protection while the latter operates from control—both signaling low awareness and energetic integration. In contrast, an Aligned Activator and a Collective Steward not only hold awareness of their impact but also embody leadership that intentionally influences systemic innovation through resonance rather than force.

Paired with the Quantum Leadership Quadrant, Johari 2.0 layers conscious and unconscious states onto energetic operating styles. Together, they form a practical guide for navigating resistance: surfacing unseen dynamics, recognizing a leader's operating style in the moment, and choosing the most coherent way to engage—whether that means offering feedback, surfacing blind spots, or simply holding steady presence to prevent burnout and invite emergence.

Together, these two frames help us see that leadership transformation isn't simply a matter of style—it's the shift from fear-driven presence to fully integrated energetic coherence. The quadrant is less about categorizing people and more focused on guiding *your* response based on moment-to-moment energetic discernment. For practitioners, this model provides a map for navigating resistance in ways that restore coherence—both personally and within the system—while still inviting regenerative progress and innovation.

Quantum Leaders cultivate the internal capacity to determine in any given moment when, how, and with whom to engage in feedback or conflict. Energetically attuned leaders know that not all feedback is useful, not all conflict is worth entering, and discernment is a key leadership skill.

| Quantum Quadrant | Johari 2.0 Lens | Primary EnQ Signal | Approach |
|---|---|---|---|
| **Collective Steward** | **Aware + Integrated** | **High** | **Engage** |
| High Positional Authority, High Inner Coherence | Open to dialogue, serves the collective. May be misperceived due to others' fragmentation. | Stable, anchored, expansive, radiates alignment and coherence. | Leverage clarity and coherence. Fosters co-creation, reflection, and energetic resonance. |
| **Aligned Activator** | **Aware + Integrating** | **Mixed** | **Match** |
| Moderate Positional, Moderate Inner Coherence | Under pressure to perform. Sensitive to systemic misalignment. | Intention-driven but influenced by power dynamics. Coherence depends on context. | Use logic and heart. Mirror energetics. Invite reflection through example, not force. |
| **Protective Achiever** | **Unaware + Open** | **Distorted** | **Gentle** |
| Low Positional, Emerging Inner Coherence | Limited perception of systemic dynamics. Driven by fear, shame, or protection. | Reactive, guarded, narrow perspective. Slowly opening. | Offer presence without pressure. Mirror safety. Progress only with trust and timing. |
| **Detached Driver** | **Unaware + Closed** | **Low** | **Limit** |
| Variable Positional, Low Inner Coherence | Closed, defensive, and reliant on dominance to maintain control. | Disconnected, performative, forceful or coercive. Masking absence of coherence. | Prioritize energetic boundaries. Model coherence, don't chase change. |

**Johari 2.0 Application:** This table translates the Johari 2.0 model into practice, offering reflection prompts and engagement paths for each quadrant. It helps leaders expand self-awareness, engage in dialogue with curiosity, and align their energetic expression with intention.

As shown, our perspective shapes not only how we connect but the energetic quality we bring to every interaction. The more we utilize EnQ, the more we reduce unnecessary conflict and deepen emotional and energetic connection with the right people, while compassionately releasing others.

**WHETHER PRESENCE FRAGMENTS OR COHERES IS SHAPED BY HOW LEADERS MOVE BETWEEN POWER AND PRESENCE, GUIDED BY INNER AUTHORITY AND THE SYSTEMS THEY SERVE**

Meaningful connection, whether with a partner, a friend, or oneself is a reflection of our own wholeness. When we lose ourselves in jobs or relationships through codependency, people-pleasing, or defining our worth through another's perspective, we are living in misalignment—diminishing our ability to lead ourselves and our sphere of influence energetically.

When we are internally aligned, we engage from overflow—seeking mutual presence, possibility, and expansion. This is an essential distinction between secure attachment and codependency—and power over versus power with—whether in personal relationships or professional dynamics, allowing for interdependence, where connection is chosen, not clung to.

In leadership, this distinction determines whether teams operate from fear and compliance, or from creativity and trust—the energetic conditions that allow emergence and innovation to flourish.

Leadership requires discernment, knowing when it is our responsibility to intervene and when it is our responsibility to step back. There is a delicate balance between speaking truth when it is needed and allowing others the space to walk their own path.

These realizations have shaped how I now show up in relationships, no longer rushing to shield myself or others from necessary lessons but learning to hold space for the process.

---

**ENERGETIC INTELLIGENCE ISN'T JUST WHAT YOU PERCEIVE—IT'S KNOWING WHEN TO ACT, WHEN TO OBSERVE, AND WHEN TO LET THINGS PLAY OUT.**

---

My maternal grandmother loved my mother deeply, but in shielding her from consequences, she enabled decades of addiction, dysfunction, and denial.

Our role is not to take that pain away from others but to stand beside them as they move through it. I used to believe that if I saw someone heading toward destruction or acting unethically, it was my job to intercede. I misconstrued intervention for support, thinking that if I just explained, showed, or tried to fix it myself, they would eventually see it too. But the more I tried to protect, to guide, to course-correct, the more I realized that saving someone from their lessons does not serve them—it stunts them.

In corporate settings, it looks different, but the dynamic is the same. Leaders insist on reviewing every draft, weighing in on every decision, unintentionally blocking momentum. Instead of growing confident, autonomous teams, they create dependency and stagnation.

When we absorb someone else's struggles as our own, we deprive them—and ourselves—of the very experiences meant to shape them and expand our growth. There is a difference between offering support, shielding someone from their own becoming, and bypassing yours by focusing on others'.

Surrender is an act of energetic trust.

Trust that the people we care for are capable of their own growth, that every challenge carries wisdom, and that lasting transformation cannot be rushed or imposed. It must be chosen.

**Even with the best intentions, intervening too often in someone else's journey can become enabling rather than empowering—and detrimental when not rooted in coherence and mutual expansion.**

Empowerment requires trust—trust in people's potential, in *their* process, and sometimes in their missteps being a valuable part of the learning curve. The ability to offer this is rooted in your Inner Authority and Energetic Intelligence.

All of which is cultivated through the pursuit of alignment—choosing self-awareness over reaction, and integration over projection. When we anchor into our own Inner Authority, we no longer seek validation in others' behavior. Instead, we observe interpersonal dynamics through the lens of frequency, impact, and responsibility. From this grounded state, we respond more often from conscious awareness—making space for relational repair and systemic regenerative innovation. This marks the difference between entanglement (reactive) and evolution (proactive).

As we become more attuned to the frequency we transmit—through practice and repetition—EnQ strengthens and we begin to notice how it shapes the field around us. Every moment we choose coherence over control and discernment over projection, we shift the collective frequency.

Transforming ourselves provides space for the field around us to recalibrate.

---

**EVERY RELATIONSHIP IS AN ENERGETIC EXCHANGE; LEADERSHIP IS SIMPLY THE AMPLIFICATION OF THOSE EXCHANGES ACROSS WIDER SYSTEMS. OUR UNRESOLVED PAIN OR PERSONAL COHERENCE DOESN'T STOP AT THE OFFICE DOOR. IT EITHER INTENTIONALLY SHAPES CULTURE OR UNINTENTIONALLY CONTAMINATES IT.**

---

Brené Brown's research on vulnerability-based leadership shows that real resilience comes not from avoiding discomfort but from learning how to navigate it. Organizations that allow space for emotional complexity, open dialogue, and accountability foster trust, innovation, and long-term well-being.

When we see relationships as tools for internal transformation, we gain access to the next level of energetic precision: how our internal coherence and presence influences connection. By tuning our own signal before we interpret others' behavior, we first establish: *what frequency am I holding and what am I transmitting into this dynamic?*

I once watched a leader who was usually confident and high-energy suddenly shift into visible discomfort while speaking. I've also seen leaders collect valuable data but dismiss or hide it because it didn't align with the story they wanted to tell. That's the unconscious and closed state: when discomfort with reality leads to defensiveness rather than dialogue. Relational EnQ is what allows us to notice these subtle shifts—signals of an inner conflict or lack of awareness that may be influencing the field.

I now see that at multiple points, I was trying to pull leaders to my level of awareness rather than meeting them gently at their own. In hindsight, I realize I can honor where someone is without compromising the standards I hold, protecting the relationship and inviting growth at a pace they can sustain.

**Leadership is about more than results. It's the tone you set, the precedent you establish, and the message your presence communicates—through policy, practice, and the field you cultivate.**

Long before I had the words for it, my body learned to track energy as a survival skill. I had to sense the shift in a room before the yelling started. I learned to read micro expressions, shifts in energy, and tension the moment it hit the air.

That sensitivity came with me into corporate America and I learned over time that the energy you bring to a room says more about your leadership than any title ever could.

When I was in the thick of excavating, repatterning, and recalibrating—working through trauma, nightmares, and flashbacks—I noticed something subtle but consistent. People responded to me differently depending on my demeanor that day. If I was calm, grounded, open: they leaned in. If I was on edge, foggy, dysregulated: they pulled back. People didn't respond to what I said; they responded to how I showed up. *Conscious attunement* and *self-regulation* is the practice of Energetic Intelligence and Quantum Leadership.

I hated knowing my team might walk into a room and spend the first five minutes trying to read me instead of focusing on their work or feeling safe because *I* was energetically unsettled. Once I realized this, I felt that the responsible thing to do was minimize the "blast radius." So I made a conscious choice to step out of leadership and into an individual contributor role.

I stopped seeing healing and leadership as two separate tracks and started seeing the truth: your personal work becomes professional impact.

Transforming ourselves transforms the world. If you aspire to lead, you don't just owe people physically tangible outcomes and bottom-line results. You owe them your coherence.

Your tone. Your regulation. Your example.

Relationships are energetic exchanges that shape and influence the collective field. Every connection, whether fleeting or profound, carries an energetic imprint that ripples beyond the individuals involved. The frequency we hold within ourselves affects the dynamic of our relationships, and in turn, those relationships reflect and reinforce our energetic state.

Interpersonal Energetics isn't about managing how others show up—it's an awareness of, and intentional care for, the energetic impact of our own presence in every connection.

Transformation happens both within and between people. When we embrace vulnerability, we create space for deeper connection. When we expand self-awareness, we reduce unnecessary conflict.

When we take responsibility for how we show up in relationships, we step into energetic sovereignty, leading not by force but by the integrity of our presence. We step into a greater responsibility: to lead not just through words or actions but through the frequency we embody.

**When we learn to hold our own energy with integrity, we stop outsourcing power and begin leading through presence, inner alignment, and embodied coherence.**

Quantum Leadership requires leading from Inner Authority—through grounded, coherent presence and a regulated system—intentionally guiding recalibration to enable growth and emergence.

Every moment of internal activation is a zero point—a chance to recalibrate, elevate, and expand the energetic impact of your presence. This is your zero point—the moment you stop outsourcing your truth and start leading from it.

Old patterns lose their grip, and a new way of being takes root. From here, every choice is a conscious creation. Every signal, every friction point, is no longer a warning to retreat but an invitation to rise.

In each moment, we are invited to ask: *am I still aligned with my unique blueprint, mission, purpose?*

### BLINK

*I moved to Spokane the summer before college. It was my last attempt at connecting with my mom. I think my eighteen-year-old brain also wanted to understand what the draw was to that kind of life. Long story short, after a couple of weeks, I confirmed her way of life was as big of a disaster as ever, and I didn't want any part of it. I got a job and moved to Yakima to live with my grandma before I left for college.*

### BLINK

It's move-in day! My mom joins my grandma and me on the drive to Bellingham. They drop me and my stuff off at my dorm room. Quickly.

A roommate's parents took us out for dinner. I thought that was super sweet. It felt normal. I was envious. Two parents? Who love and care for you? Wow.

The next day I went to go buy books and a couple of items at the bookstore. My card was declined. Odd. I knew I had money in there. I'd been saving for months. Somebody had stolen my card info and my money. I had no money, and I was completely on my own.

### BLINK

Nineteen. By all accounts, it's just another day in my Kappa Kappa dorm. Except I'm frozen, staring at the test. I'm tender. Late. The second faint line appears.

*I quickly decided that the most logical thing for me to do was move back to Spokane. I transferred to Eastern Washington University and got an apartment overlooking the river, near the local community college. It seemed like we were going to do all right. I had such high hopes for him, for us. I knew where I was headed and wanted so badly to grow together.*

## BLINK

Nearly two weeks overdue, this is my last weekend to go into labor naturally.

After twenty-plus hours of labor and an emergency C-section, I hear her cry at 3:10 p.m.

I see her eyes and touch her tiny fingers for the first time. The reality of the ways in which my life has just changed wash over me as I hold her close.

# ZERO-POINT ALIGNMENT

*"The future of Organization Development belongs to methods that affirm, compel, and accelerate anticipatory learning involving larger and larger levels of collectivity."*
—DAVID COOPERRIDER

I thought healing was something I could achieve. Some pinnacle I could reach after enough therapy, breakthroughs, and moments of clarity. But transformation isn't a place you arrive at; it's a way of life. It's an ongoing process: understanding yourself, managing your nervous system, and making daily choices that support your well-being and your most aligned, authentic self.

In quantum physics, *zero-point energy* refers to the field of pure potential. The baseline of all possibility. It is the moment we pause, align, and choose to act from our most authentic energetic frequency rather than from fear or fragmentation. A quantum unit is the tiniest possible measurement in a system. By this logic, every day we are presented with hundreds to thousands of opportunities in each decision point to obtain and maintain coherence.

Alignment is living, leading, and making decisions from deep energetic integrity rather than fear, reactivity, or for validation.

**The zero point is a charged state beneath form, where anything is possible.**

While IQ and EQ help us understand emotions and SQ anchors us in purpose, EnQ is what allows us to sense, shift, and align the energetic field connecting all of those. It's not just what we feel or believe but how we respond to and harmonize with the space around us. When we align within, we influence far more than our own path; our coherence shapes the field we share.

Leadership—of self or others—does not force change. It embodies it.

By regularly realigning our values and actions with our Inner Authority, using EnQ, we conserve our life force instead of leaking it through overextension or external validation. From this frequency, new possibilities emerge.

Alignment is not just an internal state; it's the congruence between who we are, how we show up, and the impact we create. Living in alignment is about closing the tragic gap between who we say we are and how we actually move through the world. It's about everyday choices, big and small.

Every moment is a zero-point moment. A choice point in the quantum field. A micro opportunity to reset, re-attune, and co-create with Quantum Intelligence. Each small recalibration keeps you rooted in clarity, vitality, and aligned impact.

Alignment can sometimes be mistaken for influence—the urge to convince others to think, agree, or act as we do. But Quantum Leadership is rooted in alignment that begins within. We access the field through *presence*—the continual practice of returning to our own coherence so that our signal and decisions influence impact with integrity. When we intentionally act in accordance with our values and purpose, our character reflects coherence.

As leaders develop Energetic Intelligence and use it to operate in alignment with their values, character, and purpose, they synchronize their inner and outer worlds—creating coherence that flows through teams, organizations, and systems.

## ALIGNMENT IS ATTUNING YOUR INNER SIGNAL TO MATCH THE FREQUENCY OF YOUR NEXT EVOLUTION

Every time we pause, breathe, and choose alignment over fear, intentionality over impulse, we return to the zero point. Every decision we make from clarity instead of conditioning becomes an act of conscious co-creation. Every challenge is an invitation to realign. But without a map, most people stay stuck in survival, repeating old patterns, mistaking urgency for importance and burnout for failure.

Living in alignment is recognizing that each moment is a choice to spiral deeper into fragmentation, or to rise further into coherence, energetic integrity, clarity, and positive influence.

Alignment doesn't erase challenges; it gives you a compass to navigate through them. Sometimes the hardest part is choosing to trust the guidance we receive.

*But the choice is yours.*

The ALIGNED framework helps decode those signals into sustainable, intentional action. It is designed to bridge awareness and measurable change, each step an anchor point you can cycle through quickly, or deepen over time when activated or navigating change, guiding the shift from misalignment to Inner Authority.

This framework integrates the internal journey of transformation with the outward expression of personal growth, activating the path to Quantum Leadership. This helps us turn moments of misalignment, friction, or reactivity into intentional recalibration, and allows us to return to coherence internally before engaging outward. As more people repair fragmentation, their conscience will no longer allow them to make business decisions that harm others—especially in power and leadership.

|  | Personal | Professional |
|---|---|---|
| **Awareness** | Notice when you're fragmented or reactive; pause to tune in to inner signals. | Identify cultural or systemic misalignments; surface what's unsaid, unseen, or unheard. |
| **Leadership** | Lead yourself first; embody integrity even when no one is watching. | Influence through presence to model coherence and consciously direct energy. |
| **Intentionality** | Make conscious choices aligned with your truth, not fear or old patterns. | Align decisions with purpose and values; avoid reactive or false urgency. |
| **Growth** | Lean into discomfort as a path of expansion; integrate lessons learned. | Create environments that foster learning, resilience, and regenerative innovation. |
| **Navigation** | Trust your inner compass; course-correct when you drift from alignment. | Steer teams and systems through change with clarity; reorient strategy when off track. |
| **Embodiment** | Live your values daily; coherence between head, heart, and horizon. | Translate strategy into aligned behaviors and consistent practices. |
| **Discernment** | Release what's not yours; choose what sustains alignment and well-being. | Weigh long-term alignment over short-term gains; act from integrity. |

**The ALIGNED Framework—Personal and Professional Application:** This table translates the ALIGNED framework into daily practice, showing how each pillar applies personally and professionally. It supports leaders in noticing and navigating misalignment, recalibrating with intention, and aligning values with impact.

The framework represents personal evolution and energetic recalibration from inner truth to outward impact—providing a structured, intentional approach to self-leadership, transformation, and ethical influence. It is not a one-time fix but a continual practice, inviting you to notice friction, pause, and recalibrate so your actions flow from alignment.

In practice, we live out the ALIGNED pillars in an emergent process. Whether we're facing a personal breakdown or a moment of everyday frustration, the path back to alignment often begins with activation—a moment of friction—that invites us to pause, reflect, and determine the path forward.

It is designed to help individuals and leaders recognize where misalignment is showing up by assessing actions, values, leadership approach, and growth opportunities. The process begins with building new awareness and responding intentionally to internal signals—recognizing what is yours, what is not, and how to move forward from regulated coherence. Over time, this rhythm strengthens self-trust, deepens integrity, and expands your capacity to leverage Energetic Intelligence.

In addition to being an individual integrative tool, it can be applied to guide people and organizations through friction, inertia, and misalignment. On a personal level, it offers self-reflection and coaching to uncover limiting beliefs, reconnect with purpose, and cultivate the energetic habits that support self-actualization. In leadership and organizational settings, it is designed to keep the field rooted in humanity, ethical impact, and personal accountability, helping leaders build decision-making models that prioritize long-term alignment over short-term wins.

Personally or professionally, ALIGNED is a compass that guides purpose-driven action while navigating subtle and overt resistance. It offers practical steps for integrating Quantum Leadership and Energetic Intelligence into your business, career, and life. It can be used to prevent or recover from burnout, or as a diagnostic and dialogic approach to navigating team, organizational, and systemic dynamics toward emergent, co-creative solutions.

As a field, Organization Development has long sought to balance theory and practice, wrestling with how best to support human systems in times of change, and whether the best path forward lies in diagnostic rigor or dialogic emergence. The ALIGNED model integrates both—intuitive and logical, structured and emergent.

|  | Diagnostic | Dialogic |
|---|---|---|
| **Awareness** | Identify challenge, misalignment, or pain point. | Surface unspoken truths and narratives. |
| **Leadership** | Assess influence and accountability. | Hold the field to invite collective expansion. |
| **Intentionality** | Define goals and strategic direction. | Clarity through shared values and purpose. |
| **Growth** | Address skill gaps or structures. | Facilitate becoming, emergence. |
| **Navigation** | Define roles, processes, and direction. | Sense, adapt, and co-create the path forward. |
| **Embodiment** | Align behavior to goals and roles. | Model the future through present action. |
| **Discernment** | Use data to decide what's working. | Use ethical energetic intelligence to choose. |

**ALIGNED Diagnostic and Dialogic Application:** This table compares two approaches to alignment—diagnostic and dialogic—illustrating how the ALIGNED model bridges analysis with activation. It helps leaders move from identifying dysfunction to facilitating emergence and transformation.

ALIGNED helps individuals and systems integrate fragmentation, transmute friction, and operate from a coherent core. Like Kurt Lewin's work in field theory and group dynamics, ALIGNED views change as systemic and relational. But where Lewin focused on observable behavior and environment, this framework also integrates the energetic and unseen dimensions that shape personal alignment and field dynamics. It is grounded in systems and field theory yet spacious enough for emergent, quantum possibility.[49]

ALIGNED guides you through tuning in to the unseen dynamics that shape whether change fragments or coheres. It strips away illusion, performance, and unsustainable striving, inviting us to pause and return to center—calling us back into alignment with our head, heart, and the horizon we're shaping.

**Alignment is not a one-time decision; it's a lifelong practice.**

Transformation requires a radical shift in how we relate to ourselves. It requires that we stop treating the body like a machine built for output and start honoring it as a wise partner in leading us through life.

For years, I lived in constant oscillation between trauma response. Outwardly, I could function; inwardly, my nervous system never felt safe. The signs were subtle—chronic muscle tension, shallow breathing, a low hum of anxiety—and easy to ignore until they tipped into shutdown.

Learning to recognize what state your body is in (increasing awareness) allows you to make intentional decisions (take aligned action) to process and release what is necessary in that moment (recalibrate).

These felt energetic signatures influence how we think, feel, act, and impact others. Embodiment is how we feel our way into alignment—how we know when we're aligned or misaligned. The body guides us back to intentional co-creation from the zero point again and again: the moment where choice, clarity, and creation converge.

Embodiment is how we feel our way into alignment; tuning in to the body is where transformation begins.

I used to think of my body as something separate from me. Something I needed to control, to discipline, to manage. But now I understand my body as an active participant in my transformation.

The body *holds* the data: your fascia and nervous system register coherence or misalignment before the mind can name it. This is where EnQ lives—learning to interpret signals from the quantum field through somatic intelligence, not just cognitive logic. When you tune in, fatigue, tension, tightness, and *just knowing* are no longer symptoms—they're reliable guidance.

Your nervous system, thoughts, and emotions all emit signals that influence your reality. When we are calm and regulated, we make aligned choices. But when we are stressed, dysregulated, or reactive, we reinforce cycles of misalignment.

Self-awareness, reflection, energetic attunement, emotional processing, visualization, and aligned action are tools that help you tune in to the field. When practiced consistently, they reveal breadcrumbs of information the field leaves behind, guiding you toward coherence.

When fragmented parts begin to realign, our speed and ability to discern whether people, opportunities, or our own actions are aligned or misaligned improves. You reclaim your power and access the zero point consciously, becoming *sovereign*. No longer reacting from fear, conditioning, or trauma, you begin co-creating your reality from a place of clarity and wholeness. That kind of personal power can be deeply unsettling to systems built on compliance, urgency, and disconnection because it removes their leverage.

An individual grounded in zero-point power no longer seeks external validation.

They choose consciously, morally, and ethically.

They become immune to manipulation, coercion, or manufactured urgency.

In a world where conformity fuels systemic stagnation, authentic sovereignty is a necessary form of rebellion.

Alignment isn't static; as we cycle through life's phases, each energetic shift helps repair fragmentation, strengthen coherence, and increase our ability to regulate our own signals and frequency. Energetic fluctuations are data, illuminating misalignment between what we value and how we show up. Energetic Intelligence is the ability to interpret both seen and unseen signals as quantum information—guidance revealing where we are out of sync with our truth.

**The ALIGNED framework is a bridge.**

It invites us to meet misalignment or burnout with compassion and curiosity, and to ask, *what is my soul asking me to restore?*

It guides us from activation to awareness, depletion to discernment—helping us listen to our internal signals, recalibrate our energy, and choose the most aligned next step from coherence.

## CHOICE IS POWER—CONSCIOUS, ALIGNED CHOICE IS QUANTUM LEADERSHIP

We live in a world that profits off our disconnection—from ourselves, from each other, and from our power. A world that conditions us to believe that burnout is a badge of honor, that self-sacrifice is noble, that our worth is tied to what we produce rather than who we are.

When we face and integrate our internal conflicts, that energy becomes a catalyst for personal and relational clarity, and for taking action aligned from our Inner Authority.

Quantum physics suggests that your focus determines reality, meaning that the more you attune to inner alignment and energetic coherence, the more your external world—the field—begins reflecting those truths back to you.

**Intentional alignment is how you show up for yourself, every single day.**

The more aligned we are, the more our present purpose is effortlessly revealed.

Often, the path begins with tuning in to your basic needs. *Where am I still out of alignment? What would it look like to reclaim myself fully?* Instead of reacting with overcorrection or control, the key is to reconnect with yourself and return to your *inner* guidance.

**Coherence isn't something we acquire; it's something we return to.**

At some point in every journey you realize: nothing was ever random. The experiences, the people, the detours—they were all leading you somewhere. It's just that sometimes it's impossible to see the bigger picture while you're still inside it.

As soon as I created space—as soon as I truly processed the pain and pent-up energy—my promotion path opened. But getting there wasn't about forcing or chasing. It required surrender and energetic alignment. I had to stop intellectualizing my pain, stop trying to "fix" it through logic, and instead feel it fully.

The emotions I had been suppressing—grief, anger, frustration—needed to be acknowledged and recalibrated, not analyzed. I practiced radical acceptance, not for what happened but for how it shaped me, letting go of self-blame and self-hatred. As long as I carried those weights, I was keeping myself energetically tethered to the past.

**Quantum Leaders aren't reacting to the present; they're actively co-creating the future.**

I always knew I wanted to expand beyond what I had been born into—go to college, become a business leader, then an educator. I was obsessed with books, with knowledge, always looking for insight to confirm my intuition. I knew wishing my way into a better life wasn't enough; I had to equip myself and move with intention to navigate a world that was not built for me.

In the process, I got pregnant, left an abusive relationship without a job, and became homeless with an infant. It's easy to talk about alignment when life is good. But what about when you're exhausted, uncertain, and running out of options?

Getting my degree wasn't just a personal goal. It was a refusal to accept the trajectory that had been laid out for me and that I narrowly avoided repeating.

I refused to accept failure.

Through Next Generation Zone, a workforce program for underserved youth in Spokane, I landed an internship opportunity with System Transport.

But a permanent position wasn't guaranteed.

I couldn't renew my apartment lease without proof of ongoing income. For weeks, while couch surfing and hotel hopping, I showed up every day determined to earn that spot—knowing *everything* depended on it. Each night, I would reflect and rewire while searching for apartments, as if I could have any one I wanted. I aligned my actions with my vision and followed the inner signals from my mind, body, and soul.

Time was ticking, my credit cards were maxed out, and I was slowly running out of options. One morning, my manager pulled me into a conference room to review my performance during the internship. I don't remember anything she said until, "…and we would like to offer you a permanent role."

Instant relief. I could breathe—and go get an apartment.

Landing the job at System marked the turning point. I had stable income, and we finally had a place to live. At multiple points in my life, co-creation wasn't a luxury—it was pure survival. I was working *with* the field to navigate my circumstances.

As I was finishing my undergraduate degree, I had a conversation with the head of HR, who had all but guaranteed in writing that once I graduated, they'd substantially increase my salary.

As that time neared, I sensed it wasn't going to happen. The conversations shifted. The certainty faded. I wasn't about to wait for someone else to determine my destiny again—I started looking elsewhere.

Almost immediately, an opportunity with Amazon appeared.

The morning after my interview—I got the call. I got the job. The offer was exactly what I wanted, *and then some*.

It wasn't coincidence. It wasn't luck. It was belief, persistence, and trusting the nudges that were guiding me all along.

**It was co-creation in action—preparation, persistence and *quantum alignment*—it was Energetic Intelligence.**

As my career progressed, so did the weight of the fragmentation I was masking—regular reflection and EnQ allowed me to recognize misalignment early, recalibrate quickly, and take action from coherence.

Using Energetic Intelligence and the steps outlined in this framework, I navigated a re-org that could have ended my Amazon career early, but I was tuned in and already had a new role offer when reductions on my team were announced. That decision led to my L7 promotion and solidified my role as an Organization Development practitioner.

**When we become aligned leaders in our own lives, we shift the collective.**

As more people choose alignment over avoidance, and wholeness over performance, we create a world where ethical decisions become the norm, not the exception. But it starts with each of us returning to coherence—for ourselves and for our sphere of influence.

While Quantum Strategy describes the philosophy of leading through energetic coherence, ethical influence, and systemic awareness, ALIGNED offers a step-by-step path for living that philosophy daily. The ALIGNED framework operationalizes Quantum Leadership—helping people, leaders, and teams ensure that strategic planning and systemic evolution are guided by ethical intentions and collective impact.

This framework is a real-time map for when you feel activated and want to pause before responding; when you keep burning out in the same pattern and don't know why; sense a shift emerging but doubt if it's *safe* or *right*; or when you are simply ready to stop forcing and start flowing.

*This* is how you tune in to the quantum field and take aligned action from the zero point.

## BLINK

Twenty-one. Shortly after my daughter is born, her father and I move into a different apartment, a nicer part of town in North Spokane.

*Our paths had been diverging for some time. We settled into our routines. I was comfortable focusing on undergrad and staying home with Oaklie. His job began to require travel. Distance grew. My influence faded. His true being, perhaps his trauma and pain, took hold and I began to lose him.*

Oaklie's first birthday is just the inflection point.

*I couldn't even tell you what started it.*

He's drinking heavily. His mom cuts him off at the restaurant where we have her party. He gets upset. We leave separately, and I get back to the apartment just a few minutes before him. I barely have time to get into the house. I set Oaklie down in her carrier, by the hall to our bedroom.

When he comes in, I can tell he's angrier than when we left the restaurant. In an effort to diffuse, somehow I only anger him more. Oaklie and I are directly across from him. He grabs a thin stand-up fan and throws it at me, narrowly missing her.

I'm livid. "What the FUCK is wrong with you?" I say, marching toward him.

*His eyes changed.*

He grabs me by my throat and throws me over the couch. I get up, and get right back into his face. He grabs my throat again and throws me against the front door, knocking the wind out of me. I feel my feet losing touch with the ground.

I stare into dead eyes, realizing he's lifting me higher and higher. I can't breathe. The pressure on my neck is crushing, and my vision begins to fade, darkness creeping in from every corner.

This is it…he's going to kill me.

I stop fighting and he lets me go. He runs out the sliding glass door and takes off. I don't see him again until court.

## BLINK

"I don't think he meant it, it was an accident"—excuse after excuse.

*I gave my report, weeping through hot tears, trying to justify what happened. Probably for myself more than anything.*

The officer looks up from his notepad, sees my pain and meets it with compassion. He looks me in the eyes and speaks love into my heart.

*I don't remember what he said, but I do I remember the warmth, comfort, and sudden lack of guilt I felt for getting my ass kicked.*

In less than thirty seconds the officer changed my perspective—changed my life.

## BLINK

Roughly three and a half years later—the day after I get back from Indianapolis and my interview with Amazon—I'm driving to work, torn between trusting what's meant to be and *really* wanting this opportunity to come to fruition.

My phone rings, so I pull into the parking lot of the McDonald's right by the office. It's my recruiter. "I have good news!"

*For years, I carried this vision quietly. With my own apartment came space to dream again—finish undergrad, then become a businesswoman. Independent. Successful. I pictured myself in a city, thriving in a career I loved, making real money, and becoming the person I needed to be to build something bigger than myself. I could feel it, the life I was determined to create waiting for me on the other side. Now was the time.*

# EMBODY

>>>>>>>

ASSESS BEHAVIOR AGAINST ALIGNED VALUES, CHARACTER, AND STATED MISSION

# 11

# TIDES OF TRANSFORMATION

*"The most effective people are those who can 'hold' their vision while remaining committed to seeing current reality clearly."*
—PETER SENGE

When enough people embody a different way of living and leading, the systems that once seemed unshakable will give way to new models rooted in coherence and humanity.

We spend our whole lives trying to escape suffering, but I've learned that leaning into acceptance and surrender is the fastest way through it. I always considered myself the strong one, the one who didn't need anyone. But when I started peeling back the layers, I saw the truth.

I built my strength out of fear, not freedom. I learned to be independent because I was terrified of being abandoned. I learned to control because I was afraid of chaos. I armored myself in logic and intellect because uncertainty felt like a death sentence.

## THE CHOICE TO TRANSFORM OURSELVES IS THE PATH TO QUANTUM LEADERSHIP

Every decision made from alignment strengthens your Inner Authority. You become a walking tuning fork—anchored, attuned, and available for inspired action.

At the very beginning of this journey—when everything felt uncertain, when surrender was my only option—I received a message.

*Meet me in the water.*

It wasn't loud or forceful. It was simple. Clear.

A quiet invitation.

I didn't know where it would lead, but I emphatically agreed to follow the current.

I thought I was ready to leave Amazon in 2024, but I felt the field calling me to surrender to a path that made absolutely no sense to me at the time.

I spent my whole life preparing, analyzing, ensuring that every step was calculated before I took it. Perfectionism, the illusion of control, had always been my shield against the unknown. I waited—for clarity, certainty, the perfect moment that never seemed to arrive.

The voice was gentle. It wasn't demanding or forceful. It didn't push me. It simply invited.

*Meet me in the water.*

A deep, energetic appeal to the zero point—a call into conscious awareness. I had to decide between continuing to force, or finally surrendering—releasing the shore of certainty and trusting the current to take me where I couldn't yet fathom.

I was being offered another role at Amazon. A loud part of me didn't want to take it; another part of me knew I needed to trust what I couldn't see or fully understand. I vacillated between full confidence and lingering fear before committing.

Deep down I knew it wasn't a detour; it was just part of the path.

*"Meet me in the water"* was my subconscious giving me a metaphor for entering the zero point from grounded presence and energetic clarity, where multiple probabilities collapse into the one reality that I'm willing to fully choose. It's the threshold where personal surrender meets the quantum current, and new outcomes become available.

Surrendering to the tides of transformation is flowing with Quantum Intelligence—where your thoughts, actions, and energy move in coherence. Your inner frequency and your outer life stop fighting each other and begin to move in the same direction.

Quantum Leadership doesn't come from performing harder. It comes from being honest about the signals we've ignored, and choosing alignment over achievement at all costs.

Energetic alignment feels like body, mind, and spirit finally lining up. It's a deep inner knowing that overrides logic. Your breath slows, shoulders drop, and awareness sharpens. It's the same sensation before a life-altering conversation, making a bold move, or choosing a new path—a calm, grounded certainty that you're exactly where you need to be.

Energetic Intelligence allows us to act in real-time alignment, transcending the echo of suppression with embodied self-leadership, ensuring that what we transmit is no longer fragmentation but coherence and possibility. When we transform the level of self and reclaim our Inner Authority, we interrupt that pattern.

We've been surviving a war we can't name—a war of fragmentation. Now we're being called to rebuild the systems that keep this war going. Transforming society begins with transforming how we live and lead. Even the most calcified systems are no match for a person rooted in presence, wholeness, and personal truth.

**Collective transformation starts with individual transformation.**

The world changed after World War II. A global reset in power, economy, and culture shaped the next era of human development, pushing people and societies into an entirely new relationship with work, identity, and meaning.

Before then, much of life was dictated by survival. National stability, economic security, and traditional family structures formed the backbone of Western society. But as the decades unfolded, the world shifted from collective survival to personal ambition, and from community-based resilience to hyper-individualism.

In the postwar years, Viktor E. Frankl's *Man's Search for Meaning* became one of the most defining psychological works of the time, arguing that suffering itself could be transformed into purpose. Frankl, a Holocaust survivor, saw firsthand how those who found meaning in even the most horrid circumstances were able to withstand unthinkable suffering. His research became a cornerstone of existential psychology, advancing the idea that we are not just shaped by external conditions but by the stories we tell ourselves.

Around the same time, Abraham Maslow introduced his hierarchy of needs, theorizing that once basic survival is met—food, water, security, and belonging—self-actualization becomes the next step in human development. This marked a radical shift in how people viewed fulfillment. No longer was life simply about getting by; it was about self-discovery, creative expression, and personal mastery.

Maslow's hierarchy of needs is one of the most well-known models of human development, but many don't know that Maslow drew inspiration from the Siksikaitsitapi (Blackfoot Confederacy) way of life that prioritizes community actualization over personal achievement. While both describe stages of growth, they differ in their end goal. Maslow's model moves toward individual actualization, while the Blackfoot model emphasizes reciprocity, interdependence, and collective well-being as the pinnacle of human development, challenging the notion of isolated self-improvement.[50]

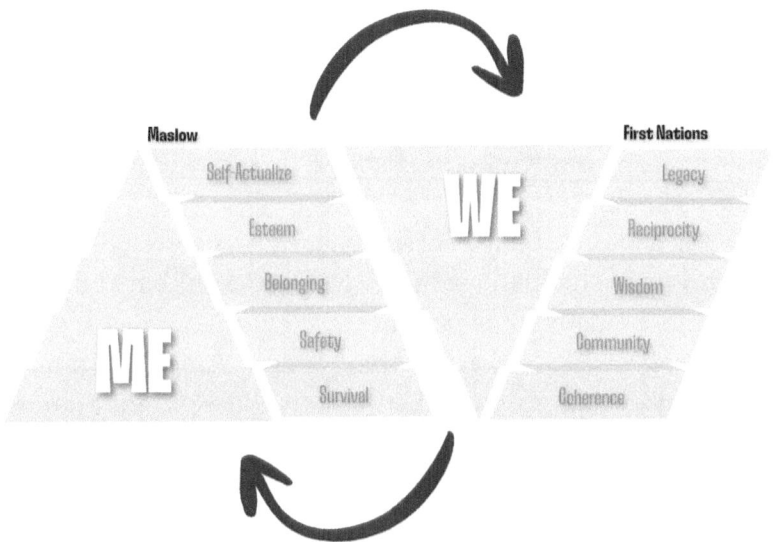

**Personal and Collective Transformation:** Where Maslow's model centers on individual attainment and actualization (the journey of "Me"), Indigenous teachings often prioritize inherent worth, interdependence, and stewardship (the journey of "We").

This inverted pyramid reflects an energetic and philosophical shift—from surviving and striving for individual success, to embodying co-creation, knowledge-sharing, and the pursuit of collective well-being across time. Both offer valuable insights, but the future of leadership demands a synthesis: recognizing that true actualization is not only about fulfilling personal potential, but about honoring and advancing the collective.

Since WWII, we've lived under the energetic residue of a survivalist paradigm—where power has been preserved through control, conformity, and competition. We are currently witnessing the attempt to hang on to this antiquated model via global resurgence of authoritarianism—marked by restrictive and regressive policies, the erosion of democratic norms, and an emboldening of leaders who consolidate power by exploiting fear, division, and disorientation.

In the decades following WWII, the fabric of collective society began to fray. As individualism skyrocketed, loneliness and disconnection followed. Robert Putnam's research in *Bowling Alone* found that civic engagement plummeted in the latter half of the twentieth century. Fewer people were joining community organizations, voting in elections, or participating in social clubs.

What had once been a society built on shared responsibility and belonging has become one of personal ambition and silent suffering. Even in corporate spaces, Christopher Lasch's *The Culture of Narcissism* warned that modern American culture encourages self-absorption, performative success, and transactional relationships.[51] The result? More people chasing external validation, yet feeling more emotionally unfulfilled than ever before.

We've drifted from that fleeting sense of shared humanity into an era defined by fragmentation. Economic shifts, political upheaval, and corporate restructuring gave rise to hyper-individualism—a culture that prized personal success over collective well-being. Our culture rewards the performance of self-actualization more than the lived embodiment of it. Many are awakening to a deeper purpose, yet struggling to fully integrate it, projecting wholeness outward while bypassing the inner reconciliation it requires, leaving us vulnerable to leaders who promise unity but prey on disconnection.

Richard Sennett's research in *The Corrosion of Character* describes how work and social structures changed after the war, shifting from long-term, stable career paths to a high-turnover, high-pressure system that prioritizes profit and efficiency over human connection.[52] Systems harden; policies prioritize productivity and consolidation of power over people. Leadership models mirror trauma more than truth, and suddenly that fragmentation has morphed into a cold civil war of ideology, identity, and individualism.

The cost of ignoring our internal fragmentation has perpetuated an explosion of burnout, detachment, and disconnection—symptoms of a world that has forgotten how to balance external achievement with internal alignment. The way forward depends on intentional leadership and use of power, grounded in ethical Energetic Intelligence and personal alignment.

---

**WHILE SOCIETY MOVED FORWARD INTO AN ERA OF TECHNOLOGICAL AND ECONOMIC PROGRESS, PSYCHOLOGICAL PROGRESS LAGGED. WE HAVE INHERITED INSTITUTIONS THAT REWARD DISCONNECTION—FROM OUR BODIES, OUR COMMUNITIES, AND OUR COLLECTIVE SOUL.**

---

While the workforce adapted, one thing remained unchanged: people still craved safety, connection, and meaning. Workplace culture evolved, but psychological safety did not keep pace with economic progress. Amy C. Edmondson's research in *The Fearless Organization* found that the highest-performing teams weren't necessarily the most talented or experienced but rather the ones where people felt safe to speak up, make mistakes, and challenge the status quo without fear of retribution.

When Google's Project Aristotle studied what made teams effective, psychological safety was the most important factor—outranking intelligence, seniority, or even technical expertise.

Edgar Schein's organizational culture theory reinforced this, demonstrating that *leadership* shapes culture more than any other factor. Leaders who encouraged transparency, vulnerability, and open communication built resilient, high-performing teams. Those who led through fear, control, or unchecked ego created fragile, dysfunctional environments.

The research is clear: societies and workplaces that value control over connection struggle with burnout, disengagement, and emotional detachment—but those that prioritize trust, psychological safety, and meaning flourish.

## HEALING DOES NOT STOP WITH THE SELF

It transforms into something greater—into service, into leadership, into shaping a world where others can heal too.

When leaders embody alignment, the shift is palpable. I witnessed firsthand Amazon's cultural shift away from the "anytime feedback" model toward a more structured system like Forte—only to watch that progress backslide under Andy Jassy, whose policies prioritized control and cost over agency and autonomy.

Notably, Jeff Bezos's approach to Wall Street is another good example of the far-reaching effects of Inner Authority and positional power. He refused to play to their quarterly demands, held fast to his long-term vision and the belief that "entrepreneurs must be willing to be misunderstood for long periods of time." That allowed him to shield Amazon's culture from short-term pressures and empower leaders closest to the work to make independent decisions—using data *and* anecdotes. Under Andy Jassy, the focus has shifted toward cost-cutting and appeasing traditional investor expectations—blanket mandates, centralized control, and rigid return-to-office policies that have disproportionately impacted women and other historically excluded people.

Where Bezos trusted the long game, Jassy has tightened the reins, prioritizing immediate compliance over cultural coherence. We will observe the effects for years to come.

**True self-actualization is not an individual pursuit but a communal responsibility.**

We cannot move forward unless we reconcile the wounds of the past—both individually and as a society. The unwillingness to acknowledge wounds on a personal level creates the same resistance to repair and reconciliation at a collective level.

Societies deny, project, and avoid their own shadows in the same way individuals do. The way we repress, deny, and avoid within ourselves is the same way institutions, communities, and societies perpetuate dysfunction. When we begin to integrate our shadows, we not only change ourselves; we shift the energetic landscape around us.

These shifts aren't just political. They're energetic. The more we collectively shift into attunement and coherence, the less fragmentation fuels fear-based systems.

The water—the unknown, the flow of life—was never meant to be figured out before stepping in. It was meant to be entered, experienced, *felt*. Let go of the familiar shore—the safety of what you've always known—and allow yourself to be carried into something greater.

The brain is wired to conserve energy by relying on established patterns and deeply engrained neural pathways, which is why breaking out of familiar behaviors—no matter how unfulfilling—feels so unnatural. Disrupting old neural connections requires effort, intention, and repetition before new habits feel automatic.

Perception of difficulty often deters people too. Many tend to overestimate the effort required to start a new habit but underestimate the long-term benefits of consistency.[53]

Beyond neuroscience and behavioral patterns, change is emotionally disruptive. Transformation forces us to confront what is no longer working—and that means acknowledging discomfort, fear, and uncertainty.

Transformation is not a one-time event but a continual choice to meet yourself and others at a higher standard. Leaders who have done this work hold space for others to rise, modeling what it looks like to lead from integration and Inner Authority.

Transformation is both an internal and external process. It requires shifting belief systems, rewiring neural pathways, restructuring habits, and building the resilience to withstand discomfort. The process is uncomfortable at first—but that is not a sign to stop. It is proof that you are stepping into something new.

**Transformation is energetic recalibration.**

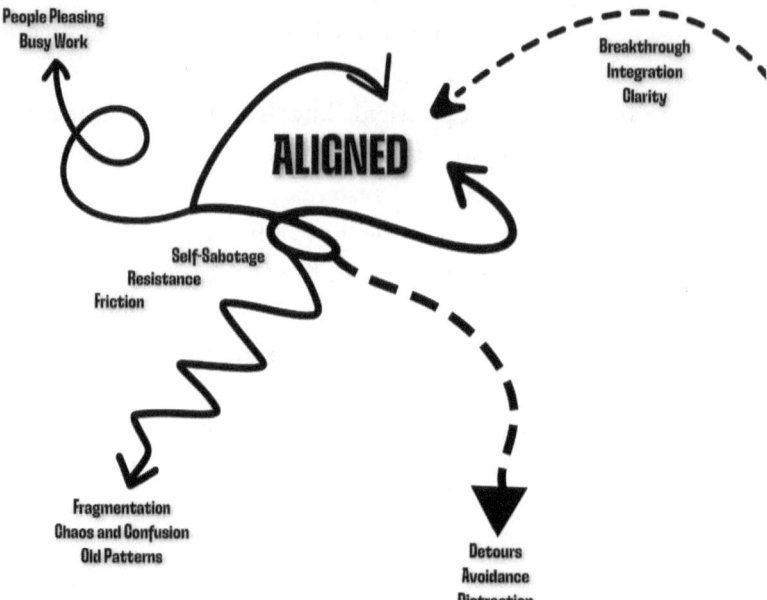

**Path to Alignment:** This image illustrates the dance between resistance and return—the way we spiral through patterns until awareness transforms friction into alignment, clarity, and flow.

*Meet me in the water.*

At the time, it felt like a reminder that I could leap without inviting chaos and without fear.

Willingly meeting the tides of transformation is about loosening your grip on the familiar. It's surrendering to movement you can't fully understand but feel is right. In that moment, clarity doesn't come before the leap; it comes because you've stepped in.

The tide meets you when you meet it.

As I witnessed the path unfolding, I realized that surrender doesn't mean losing control. It means trusting that everything is happening exactly as it should.

In the quantum field, every choice sends a signal—an energetic imprint—that reshapes what becomes possible. Surrender is not passive; it's deliberate alignment with the current of potential, where your frequency calls in the reality you're ready to fully live.

Every great shift in my life happened because I took action

before I was completely ready, and I moved urgently when my soul said *go*.

I didn't know the outcome when I left my mom at sixteen, but I trusted that a better life was possible.

I didn't know the full story of my past when I began my healing journey, but I trusted that clarity would come.

I didn't have all the answers when I left stability behind to follow my calling, but I trusted that I was being guided.

I am.

*So are you.*

I don't have some *magical* ability that you don't.

I simply *listened*. And when it was time to move, I *moved*.

Had I not taken that last role at Amazon, and surrendered to the guidance of the present moment instead of my rigid vision for the future, I would have missed out on some of the best connections I've made since the early years in Operations.

I mentored or coached over fifty different leaders from various teams and organizations across the company. I led another Organization Development initiative, and gained invaluable experience observing and navigating organizational dysfunction *using* EnQ.

From navigating a chaotic upbringing, leaving an abusive relationship, and escaping homelessness to building a career at one of the most innovative companies in the world, I relied on Energetic Intelligence to turn pain into purpose and align each step with a greater vision for my life.

It was the same clarity and confidence I drew on at critical moments as a child, then at sixteen when I moved out. I knew life without my mother was going to be better than life with her. As painful as that has been at various times, had I not listened to that, surrendered to that, I tend to believe that my life would be far different than it is today.

For more than thirty years, Energetic Intelligence has been the backbone of my approach to life and leadership—carrying me through survival, personal transformation, corporate America, and to developing Quantum Strategy.

I didn't have the full picture, but I trusted the pull, and every leap carried me further than I could have planned.

## SEPARATION IS THE ROOT CAUSE OF SUFFERING, AND PERSONAL TRANSFORMATION IS THE PATH TO COLLECTIVE REPATTERNING

The field is calling you to step into your own becoming, to embrace your journey—however messy, uncertain, and imperfect it may seem.

There may never be a moment when you arrive—because this life, this journey, is a continual unfolding, a process of meeting yourself over and over again, of shedding layers, of stepping further into alignment and surrendering to the field. Trusting that when the time comes, the tide will always be there to meet you.

To step into the unknown is to surrender the need for certainty. To admit that you don't have all the answers. To open your heart, knowing that it may break but also knowing that in its breaking, it will expand.

I spent years trying to protect myself from pain. I built walls so high that even I couldn't see over them. I mistook control for safety, perfection for worthiness, detachment for strength. But real strength—the kind that changes lives and shifts the energy of an entire room—is found in openness. In softness. In the willingness to be seen.

**In turbulent water, even truth gets distorted. In still water, we see clearly.**

At the end of 2024, the message came again: *it's time to jump.*

I knew the leap was coming—I prepared for it, co-created, did everything I could to ensure it would be a smooth transition. But now, the moment was here. Every sign, synchronicity, and instinct told me *it's time.*

It felt just like the moment years ago when I was leaving System Transport, the trucking company where I received a job offer that became my introduction to logistics, supply chain, and my first formal leadership role.

I remember lying on the couch after flying home from my interview with Amazon, feeling sorrowful and uncertain, but beneath the fear, there was a quiet knowing that everything would work out. And sure enough, the very next day, the call came. I got the job—doubling my salary overnight.

*Life-changing.*

Trusting the tide and allowing it to guide me had been worth it.

In the weeks leading up to my last day at Amazon, a major speaking opportunity came through. The deadline to accept fell on the exact same date—eleven years to the day—since I had started.

A zero-point moment, the exact convergence of ending and beginning, collapse and creation. Energy, effort, and focus compounding into a threshold moment where transformation takes root, if we choose to honor where it's calling us.

**The greatest act of courage is not in knowing the way or the why, but in taking the first step anyway.**

Every leap I've taken was more than a career move—it was a shift in the current I was aligned with. EnQ is what enables us to act from Inner Authority in real time—to sense dissonance before collapse, to course-correct without shame, and to embody aligned power, moment by moment. Trusting my Energetic Intelligence has positioned me for the experiences, challenges, and clarity I needed to lead from my purpose with full confidence.

When we ignore those internal signals, burnout and chaos are the ultimate cost.

When we honor them, transformation becomes inevitable.

When we align, we create coherence and move *with* the current—allowing the tides of transformation to *carry us* toward what serves the whole.

Every single one of us has the power to create change—not just in our own lives but in the lives of everyone we encounter. When you heal yourself, you shift the energy of every room you walk into. When you show up as your aligned, authentic self, you give permission for others to do the same.

If enough of us do that, if enough of us take ownership of our lives and start making choices based on alignment instead of fear, we *will* change the world.

You don't have to be perfect to begin. You don't have to be fearless. You just have to *be willing*.

Willing to step forward, even if your voice shakes.

Willing to embrace your truth, even if others don't understand it.

Willing to show up, again and again, for yourself and your purpose.

The energy we embody determines whether our ripples heal or harm. When our internal system is rooted in safety and coherence, our intentions carry a natural authority that inspires trust, shifts systems, and uplifts those we cross paths with.

Alignment radiates.

**BLINK**

*What does the future look like, when we lead from alignment?*
 The air is lighter.
 Decisions are made in rooms where every voice matters.
 Work feels like contribution, not survival.
 Leaders listen as much as they speak.
 Families have time together.
 Our systems nourish the people they serve.
 The tide has turned. Not because one person willed it, but because we built it together.

**BLINK**

Business, organizations, and work feel lighter. The air itself seems clearer, alive with transparency and trust.

Leaders speak less about margins and more about meaning; growth is measured in lives uplifted, communities nourished, and opportunities created. Capital still flows, but there is a greater emphasis on reciprocity, regeneration, and mutual benefit.

Success means ecosystems flourish, resources are honored rather than irresponsibly extracted, and companies become sanctuaries of coherence where value is created without depleting the soul.

Leaders ask: *who do we serve, and do our choices carry positive change?*

# 12

# QUANTUM STRATEGY

> *"You cannot change any society unless you take responsibility for it, unless you see yourself as belonging to it and responsible for changing it."*
> —GRACE LEE BOGGS

The tide is shifting. The systems we built on outdated assumptions, practices, and dogma—economically, politically, socially—are breaking under their own weight. More people are awakening to their wounds, questioning what they once accepted, and choosing to live differently—to lead differently.

Quantum Leadership is accessed through personal transformation and self-transcendence.

*Quantum Strategy* emerges when groups operate from shared coherence, achieving exponential results in record time and working for the greater good—when strategy is evaluated for human and systemic impact ahead of shareholder return.

Quantum Strategy incorporates energetics and societal progress into organizational practice—aligning leadership development, culture, and systems with collective benefit and human-centered growth. It provides leaders with tools to navigate dissonance, recalibrate patterns of power, and unlock people's fullest potential. When organizations embed Quantum Strategy, transformation moves from concept to culture—shaping environments where innovation, collaboration, and human flourishing can thrive.

As more people recalibrate their inner systems and choose to live in authentic wholeness, we will build a world that is fundamentally different. A world where leadership is rooted in consciousness, not control, and systems are designed to be human-centered, not just for profit.

## IF WE WANT TO CHANGE THE WORLD, WE MUST FIRST CHANGE THE WAY WE SHOW UP WITHIN IT

Too often, people believe that changing the world requires external action—overthrowing corrupt leaders, reforming broken systems, restructuring power. But transformation happens first within. A society built on emotional suppression, unresolved trauma, and conditioned compliance will continue to produce leaders who reflect those wounds. Our energy ripples into every room, every relationship, every system we participate in. We are always co-creating, whether consciously or not.

The current leadership crisis is not one of talent or intelligence but of energetic fragmentation and misalignment. Personal alignment isn't personal at all; it's the seed of collective evolution.

Just as an individual cannot truly thrive in isolation, collective recalibration cannot occur without individuals who are willing to do the inner work. Community is necessary for mirroring, for feedback, for integration. The key is in finding the balance, knowing when to retreat to do the inner work and when to return to let others hold a mirror to what still needs to be healed.

Systems built on disconnection depend on your misalignment.

Your clarity threatens their control. When you align, you don't just change your life—you change what the system can get away with. Burnout, widening wealth gaps, manipulative power structures, and the rise of authoritarianism are symptoms of a deeper issue: unhealed leadership acting from fear, scarcity, and ego. When those in power manipulate the human nervous system—provoking fear, creating dependency, and suppressing critical thought—they perpetuate and exploit the very systems they've been entrusted to transform.

**Alignment is the antidote. Activating your blueprint is the cure.**

Alignment isn't just about personal well-being; it's about how you engage with the world. In an era of constant information, political upheaval, and systemic challenges, it's easy to feel overwhelmed, exhausted, or paralyzed by the weight of it all. Many of us swing between hyper-engagement (doomscrolling, overconsumption of media, constant advocacy) and complete disengagement (numbness, avoidance, cynicism). But neither extreme is sustainable.

Societal transformation occurs when enough *individuals* operate from a place of conscious leadership, altering collective paradigms. The world doesn't change because of one big moment; it changes because people make different choices.

Personal and collective leadership exists in moments of reckoning, in the pause between reaction and response. In the choice to stay present with discomfort and intentionally move through it for your own growth rather than avoid it.

Quantum Leadership shapes lived reality—one recalibration, one choice, one act of alignment at a time. It amplifies inner energetic alignment, where your healed presence reveals *and* disrupts dysfunctional leadership patterns, power dynamics, societal conditioning, and outdated paradigms.

As we become more certain of our values, motivations, and intentions, we develop the ability to recognize and recalibrate fragmentation, release projections, and engage in relationships from a place of aligned Inner Authority, a place of clarity rather than fear.

**The work we do on ourselves doesn't just change our own lives—it shifts the collective.**

When we heal, we heal the field. When we rise, we create space for others to rise. The way we handle our relationships sets the energetic tone for the spaces we lead, influencing both personal and professional dynamics. When we embody the future we want to see, we become the leaders who bring that into existence.

As I strengthened my EnQ, I also deepened my ability to separate my reactions from undistorted reality. I learned to sit with discomfort rather than immediately assigning blame. I learned to ask myself if I was responding from present awareness or from past wounds.

The future of regenerative, high-impact leadership will be found in leaders who foster decentralized, adaptable ecosystems where psychological safety, collaborative intelligence, and emergent actions replace bureaucratic inefficiency and consolidated power.

Societies with extreme income inequality suffer from higher crime, weaker social trust, and declining mental health. If leaders remain unhealed, acting from scarcity, fear, and ego, they create institutions that reflect those same dysfunctions. When people lead from fear, ego, or a desire to control, they replicate the very patterns they once tried to escape.

**When we transform from the inside out, we lead and interact differently. We create a ripple effect that shifts organizations, businesses, and entire cultures.**

Systems are not broken by accident; they are a reflection of the collective state of human consciousness. Institutions are built on the beliefs of the people who design and sustain them. When those beliefs stem from survival and domination-based leadership, we create systems that mirror fragmentation: inequality, burnout, distrust, disconnection, and extraction over regeneration.

When leaders operate from Inner Authority—rooted in trust and conscious presence—they create cultures of safety, innovation, and possibility. Integration, recalibration, and full system regulation are not just personal milestones; they empower leaders, businesses, and systems to evolve.

Quantum Strategy is a commitment to our individual responsibility to uplift the collective experience of those within our sphere of influence. It is about redefining success through the lens of impact, integrity, and interconnectedness.

**Quantum Leadership is a reflection of the world we wish to create.**

A world where personal empowerment replaces external control—where leadership is driven by regeneration rather than extraction.

Every person who picks up this book is embarking on a personal and leadership development journey; one that demands higher ethical standards, conscious choices, and the courage to challenge and redesign outdated systems. This means holding businesses and corporations accountable for their impact on the world, and making intentional decisions about where we invest our time, energy, and money.

Are we fueling organizations that perpetuate inequality, exploitation, and collective regression? Or are we aligning with those who contribute to a more ethical, human-centered future?

Even when circumstances force us into environments that feel misaligned—whether for financial stability, career growth, or personal obligations—those moments present the greatest opportunities to practice Energetic Intelligence and Quantum Leadership.

We aren't fixing broken systems. We're dismantling the frequency that built them.

When leaders operate from coherence, they create ecosystems rooted in well-being, equity, and autonomy—communities grounded in shared purpose. If we want a society in which opportunity and innovation are accessible, we need leaders who embody and build those values into the systems they influence. A thriving world is one where opportunity, education, and autonomy are accessible to all. Anything less reflects collective wounding.

Quantum Leaders co-create systems that reflect shared values—embodying reciprocity, creativity, and interdependence.

**When leaders transform, societies evolve.**

For years, psychology has framed self-actualization as an individual journey. But in many Indigenous and wisdom traditions, true self-transcendence is inseparable from community well-being.

This distinction is reflected in other psychological frameworks of human growth, such as transformational leadership, Spiral Dynamics, Robert Kegan's Theory of Adult Development, and Jane Loevinger's stages of ego development. All of these models describe progressive stages of development, moving from basic survival needs to self-awareness and cognitive complexity, from individual transformation to collective transformation, from rational intelligence to intuitive intelligence.

Personal transformation and self-transcendence are not just about emotional and energetic regulation; it's about expanding awareness, shifting motivations, and ultimately pursuing a positive impact *beyond* the self.

Integration and recalibration creates internal alignment, elevating our relationships, which in turn shifts the dynamics we attract, sustain, or release. When we reclaim our Inner Authority, we show up differently, creating healthier, more conscious dynamics that carry outward into families, communities, and global systems.

## THE WORK WE DO WITHIN SETS THE STAGE FOR THE IMPACT WE HAVE ON OUR SPHERE OF INFLUENCE

David Bohm's concept of the *Implicate Order* suggests that what we perceive as separate entities—individual leaders, teams, organizations—are actually part of a deeper, interconnected whole.[54] The visible structures of leadership—decision-making, policies, corporate culture—are merely the *Explicate Order*, the surface manifestation of unseen forces like intention, energy, and belief systems. Leaders who understand this recognize that their impact extends far beyond what they say or do, that their very state of *being* influences the system around them.

Quantum *entrainment* and *entanglement* state that particles remain connected regardless of distance, offering powerful parallels for leadership. Entrainment reflects how a single coherent leader can regulate and synchronize the energy of a team in real time, while entanglement shows how their presence continues to influence behavior and outcomes even after they've left the room. When leaders are aligned—mentally, emotionally, and physiologically—their teams synchronize with that energy.

A Quantum Leader's impact does not end when they leave a role, an organization, or even this lifetime. Their influence becomes woven into the system, into the behaviors and beliefs of those they have empowered.

Some argue that direct action and decision-making are more impactful than indirect influence, particularly in high-stakes leadership environments where urgency and immediate results are required. Others caution that influence without structure or accountability can lead to charismatic leadership that lacks real substance or systemic change.

Quantum Leaders pair direct action with energetic influence.

Using intellectual, emotional, spiritual, and energetic intelligence, they take decisive action when necessary. They also recognize that their greatest power is in setting the foundation for sustained transformation long after they are gone.

Leadership is no longer just about strategy, execution, or authority; it's about consciously shaping reality. The future belongs to those who understand that leadership is a creative force—one that blends energetic alignment, strategic action, and deep self-awareness to create lasting impact.

Leaders who understand this do not chase influence. They become it. Their presence is felt, even when they are not in the room. Their impact ripples outward, shaping generations of future leaders, teams, and entire industries.

**Leadership is the environment you cultivate.**

Coherence is not passive. It's a practice. Through regulation and intentional awareness, leaders can shift their energetic imprint in real time.

The best leaders are not just intellectually strategic; they are energetically *fluent*.

They understand that leadership is not about controlling people; rather it is managing the frequency they emit—one that invites collaboration, confidence, and trust.

When a leader is in coherence, everyone around them feels it, and that is energetic influence.

When we have done the work to lead ourselves, we become conduits for something much bigger. At that point, influence isn't about ego—it's rooted in integrity. We become safe places for others to grow and expand in. Our sphere of influence begins to reflect a different kind of power.

Our culture is hungry for new systems, but those systems will not sustain unless the people within them have evolved. This happens only when we stop outsourcing leadership to titles and start claiming the responsibility we have to each other and our planet.

The process of intentional co-creation is about shifting from force to flow—from control-based manifestation (pushing, striving, overworking) to energetic alignment (trusting, allowing, acting from clarity and self-trust).

Leadership, at its most impactful, is energetic. It's not just what you say or do; it's who you are when you enter the room. It's the frequency you emit.

**Quantum Leadership requires courage, the willingness to speak up when something is unethical, misaligned, or hindering the organization's success.**

Leadership is not confined to titles; anyone within an organization can lead. A thriving society depends on individuals who challenge harmful leadership and advocate for integrity, ensuring both people and performance reach their highest potential.

The systems many of us were raised in—home, school, and institutional hierarchies—were designed to preserve control, not invite expansion. They reward perfectionism, self-sacrifice, and emotional suppression while labeling authenticity and energetic acuity as threats.

These systems normalize disconnection from self and others, often masking dysfunction as professionalism or tradition—a model designed to keep the majority in survival mode, dependent on external systems of power and validation.

But there is another way. A different way. A better way.

These patterns reward urgency over wisdom. They prize hyper-productivity over coherence. They condition us to override our inner guidance to maintain control at the cost of *our power*.

---

**WE'RE NOT HERE TO PLAY THE GAME—WE'RE HERE TO CHANGE THE FREQUENCY OF THE ENTIRE FIELD. SUCCESS IS NO LONGER ABOUT PLAYING BY THE RULES OF A BROKEN SYSTEM; IT IS ABOUT EXECUTING A VISION FOR A NEW ONE WITH UNWAVERING INTEGRITY.**

---

We have the power to reimagine society by centering humanity. As more people undergo their own personal transformation—shedding the layers of pain, fear, and trauma that breed dysfunction—they are more likely to make better choices for themselves, their communities, and the planet.

This is how we increase collective consciousness where people act in harmony with one another without the need for force or control, by transforming ourselves and our sphere of influence.

Every healed wound, every conscious interaction, every act of emotional repair lowers the collective volume of fragmentation and raises the vibration of unity, trust, and integrity.

Every time we choose to confront our own wounds rather than projecting them onto others, we shift the energetic patterns we pass forward. Every time we model healthy communication, self-awareness and emotional regulation, we teach those around us—our partners, our children, our teams—how to navigate life in a conscious, empowered way.

Reclaiming your power and your freedom is messy. Fragmentation doesn't disqualify us; it reveals what still needs compassion. Grace is not something you deserve once you've worked hard enough. It's something you integrate daily, in every setback, every moment of doubt, every time the inner critic rises.

I've learned that freedom isn't just about escaping oppression; it's about reclaiming the parts of ourselves we've been taught to shrink, submit, or suppress. It's healing what keeps us reacting from fear instead of responding from alignment.

Self-compassion is a practice, not a reward.

Studies repeatedly show that when we are regulated, our thoughts, energy, and behaviors align more easily with what we want to create. This reinforces what Carl Rogers taught for decades: sustainable transformation begins with unconditional self-regard, not external achievement. When we cultivate self-worth and coherence from within, we naturally operate from a more empowered, human-centered state—one that no longer chases validation but radiates confidence.

I spent years chasing success, thinking freedom lived in

achievement, external validation, or finally earning enough to rest. But true freedom came when I began listening to my Inner Authority. When I stopped abandoning myself in pursuit of approval. When I started choosing coherence over control.

**Alignment with yourself and in service to the collective is freedom—waking up every day feeling like you are exactly where you are meant to be, doing exactly what you are meant to do.**

Personally, freedom means listening to my body, honoring my natural cycles of rest and action, and remembering that success isn't about how much you can do. It's about how fully and authentically you can live. It won't be found in a title, a relationship, or a bank account.

Freedom is found in who you choose to become.

True freedom is about reclaiming agency over your energy, your choices, and the way you show up in the world. We become free by choosing alignment, again and again, even when it's inconvenient. We become free by honoring the truth of who we are, reclaiming our purpose, and showing up in the world with integrity.

**I used to wonder what kept my mother trapped. Now I wonder what would have freed her.**

That question has shaped every step of my own leadership journey.

You cannot meditate your way out of food insecurity, journal your way out of systemic inequities, or breathe through the stress of working multiple jobs to survive.

Whether an individual desires wealth, a comfortable middle-class life, or a simple existence, they should have the freedom to choose, without systemic barriers that force them into survival mode.

> ANCIENT WISDOM, SPIRITUAL PHILOSOPHIES, AND EMERGING RESEARCH ON COOPERATIVE ECONOMIES ALL POINT TOWARD THE SAME TRUTH: WHEN PEOPLE'S BASIC NEEDS ARE MET, WHEN THEY ARE FREE TO EXPLORE THEIR PASSIONS, CONTRIBUTE MEANINGFULLY, AND DEFINE SUCCESS ON THEIR OWN TERMS, SOCIETIES FLOURISH.

Quantum Leadership is the ability to set high standards without inducing fear. It is the embodiment of regenerative leadership, where success is not driven by force but by cultivating conditions that enable people to thrive.

Leadership is an extension of the inner world, and those who lack Inner Authority often struggle to influence ethically and sustainably. Before a leader can influence organizations, shape industries, or drive global change, they must be deeply grounded in their own personal evolution.

Energetic Intelligence is the capacity to align your internal state with the frequency of the impact you wish to create. Energetic attunement and action are not separate—they are intertwined. The process is not about blind hope; it is embodied trust—the energetic alignment of belief, emotion, and behavior.

**The ripple begins within.**

We make repeated choices to interrupt long-held momentum, shifting our energy, one thought, one step, one action at a time until healing transforms into something greater. Moving outward, from me to we, from self-preservation to service, from confusion to clarity. From survival to service.

This requires rewiring subconscious beliefs that contradict what you want to create. Releasing nervous system resistance through somatics, fascia, and embodiment work. Practicing emotional and energetic congruence, feeling as though your desires are already real, allowing the body to anchor into that frequency, and taking aligned action. When leaders embody this coherence, it shifts the entire culture they serve. Presence becomes strategy, and coherence ripples through the environment and the people in it via entrainment and entanglement.

Peter Senge's Learning Organization confirms that leaders who commit to continuous self-development don't just transform themselves; they uplift entire systems.[55] When leaders evolve, the systems they touch evolve with them. Quantum Leadership is about recalibrating yourself first, shifting the culture by embodying the frequency of what you want to create. Quantum Leaders don't just direct others; they intentionally attune the field.

Leaders rooted in EnQ and Inner Authority lead with wisdom, presence, and integrity—inviting alignment rather than imposing control. Their presence becomes a model for expansive, regenerative leadership, setting a new tone for what's possible. The future of leadership is no longer about control—it's about co-creation. The leaders who embody this will not only realize their own success; they will be the architects of a new paradigm.

The learning organization concept emphasizes the importance of shared vision, mental models, and personal mastery—all of which mirror the inner alignment required for Quantum Leadership.

**Leading through energetics and collective consciousness is a fundamental and necessary shift in how we live, lead, and interact.**

It is about choosing, every single day, to lead from coherence and alignment.

Just because "it's always been done this way" does not mean we must continue. Just because a system benefited those before us does not mean we must perpetuate harm to maintain our place within it. Every morning, you have a choice: do you remain stuck in outdated paradigms, or do you allow yourself to see a new path forward?

> **WHEN YOU PRACTICE LIVING IN ALIGNMENT, A NEW PATH BEGINS TO REVEAL ITSELF—NOT IN DISTANT, ABSTRACT POSSIBILITIES BUT IN THE DECISIONS YOU MAKE TODAY, IN THE PRESENT MOMENT.**

When you expand awareness beyond yourself, you see how small, individualized focus affects the rest of the planetary community. Suddenly, issues like privacy, free speech, and social justice are no longer just political debates; they become imperative reflections of our collective expectations for how we treat one another, and what freedom, responsibility, and honor truly mean.

Our collective call to action is not just to imagine this future but to actively co-create it. To plant the seeds of new societal structures that prioritize well-being, justice, and self-actualization over extraction and control. This begins with internal coherence. When our values, character, and energy are aligned, we don't need to force outcomes—we become the field through which they form.

There is a moment in every transformation journey where the focus shifts. At first, it was about survival, understanding your wounds, unpacking your past, healing. Then it shifts to personal achievement, self-actualization—learning how to align your life with your values, build resilience, and own your Inner Authority.

Once you have reclaimed yourself fully, what do you do with that power?

## WHEN ENOUGH LEADERS RISE INTO CONSCIOUS AND ALIGNED LEADERSHIP, WE DON'T JUST EVOLVE ORGANIZATIONS OR INDUSTRIES—WE ELEVATE HUMANITY

Leaders with strong Inner Authority trust themselves; they exude grounded, flexible confidence rooted in inner truth and collective service. Their discernment is sharp but not reactive. Their decisions are responsive, not performative.

**Without Inner Authority, positional authority risks becoming performative or oppressive. With it, leadership is regenerative, magnetic, and transformational.**

The ultimate transformation is when you realize that your growth was never just for *you*. Your healing, your journey, your story is meant to be shared in a way that *creates change*—in your home, in your community, in your workplace, and in the world.

When you reach a place of self-actualization and clarity, when you truly know who *you* are and what you stand for, you can no longer sit idly by and watch the world operate in dysfunction. You can no longer tolerate mediocrity in leadership. You can no longer accept "that's just the way things are" as an answer.

You *must* step up.

You *must* take what you have learned and use it to shape the spaces you occupy.

You *must* lead, because your integrity demands it.

The more I tried to conform, the harder leadership felt.

**Leadership is about *power and influence*. How you use each, and in service of whom, determines your impact.**

Leadership is not reserved for the few; it belongs to those who choose to show up in service of the many.

*Everyone* has influence. Everyone is leading in some way.

Your family. Your team. Your clients. Your community.

You influence your family by the way you show up in your relationships.

You influence your workplace in the way you navigate conversations and decisions.

You influence your community with the standards you set and the actions you take to help uphold those standards.

You don't have to be in a position of power to be a leader. You just have to be willing to take ownership of the spaces you are already in. When you show up differently in your family, on your team, in your community—when you embody your values consistently—that alone can change trajectories.

**You influence the world whether you intend to or not. Your presence, your choices, your energy—they echo.**

Your presence alone becomes an invitation, a call to rise, a mirror that reflects to others what is possible when they honor their Inner Authority and live in alignment with their *blueprint*.

Quantum Leadership is energetic.

Quantum Strategy emphasizes intentionally transforming activation into aligned impact—*shared power* through *alignment, coherence, and Inner Authority.*

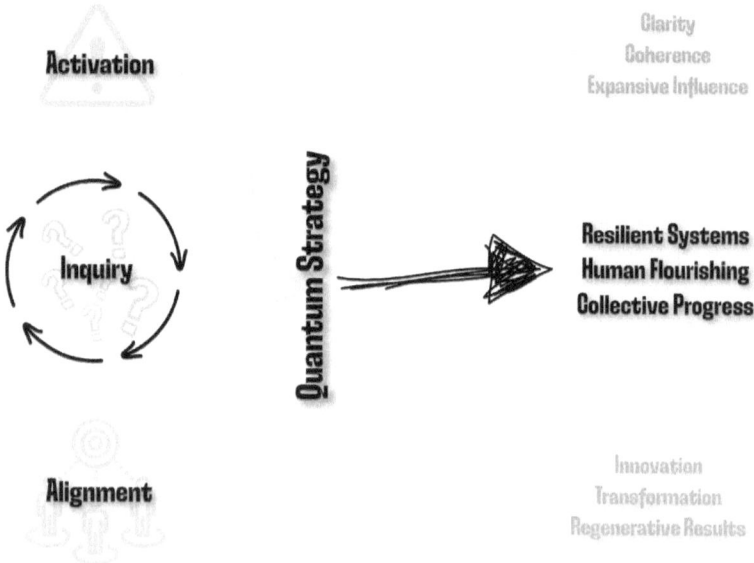

**Quantum Strategy:** Activation, Inquiry, and Alignment form a continuous cycle that translates intentional personal growth into regenerative collective impact

# BLINK

"How did you do it?"
"I didn't *do* it. I *became* it."

# DISCERN

>>>>>>>>

CONTINUOUSLY EVALUATE VIA FRICTION AND FLOW TO RECALIBRATE WHEN ACTIVATED
REPEAT AS NEEDED

# 13

# ACTIVATING YOUR BLUEPRINT

*"Knowing is not enough; we must apply.
Willing is not enough; we must do."*
—JOHANN WOLFGANG VON GOETHE

Use your experience, your wisdom. Use your voice. Use your influence. Wherever you are, however you can, for the collective benefit of all.

**When you rise, you give others permission to do the same.**

By becoming whole within ourselves, we disrupt inherited patterns and model alignment. We extend that integrity and coherence into every decision, relationship, and system we influence. Not through force, anger, or division.

**Through *example*. Through *frequency*.**

One person at a time choosing to step into their truest self and inspiring those around them to do the same. You have done the inner work; now it is time to carry that transformation forward.

This world does not need more passive bystanders. It does not need more people who are aware but unwilling to act. We need *people* who are committed to their own evolution and who use that evolution to create change in their communities, families, industries, and beyond.

The world doesn't just need healed people; it needs *healed leaders*.

**We need Quantum Leaders.**

Start by asking yourself, *what kind of energy do I bring into a room? How do I show up for others? Do I encourage them to step into their potential, or do I hold them back out of my own fear or insecurity?*

*Do my actions reflect my values, even when no one is watching?*

*Am I using my voice, or am I staying silent for the sake of comfort?*

The journey of self-transcendence and conscious leadership evolves *with* you.

Our level of awareness and consciousness determines how we engage with others, make decisions, and shape the systems around us. Every choice, every action, every zero-point moment presents an opportunity to live in alignment, lead with intention, and transform our sphere of influence.

As we evolve, so does our impact.

The world is not just changing; it is *transforming*, and it requires a new kind of leadership.

Leaders who embody alignment and coherence break cycles of dysfunction and model a new standard—where power is used to unite, advance collective progress, and reshape what business and leadership seek to accomplish across industries and institutions.

**Quantum Leaders don't just lead differently. They lead others to do the same.**

At the most fundamental level, leadership cannot be separated from human development. The way we lead—whether in organizations, communities, or our personal lives—reflects the dominant level of consciousness we operate from.

## ACTIVATING YOUR BLUEPRINT—INTENTIONALLY REALIGNING YOUR LIFE WITH YOUR PURPOSE—IS THE FOUNDATION FOR COLLECTIVE CHANGE

Personal transformation is not about perfection. It exists in the daily habits that support balance, resilience, and well-being over the long term. It comes from cultivating the ability to tune in to your inner guidance system, building sustainable, restorative practices, and living an aligned life. Resting when you need to. Pushing yourself when you should. Waking up every day, intentionally showing up in service of personal purpose and collective progress.

Activating your blueprint is coming home to the truth of your divine intelligence—your inner compass, your infinite wisdom, your personal source code.

It's not about becoming more; it's about remembering who you already are.

It's reconnecting to your deepest truth *and* to the collective field.

It's learning to distinguish your truth from what you've absorbed—learning to tune in to your internal frequency, and tune out the static. It feels like the crumbling of what you once knew, and the quiet homecoming to a peace you've long sensed but couldn't name.

Life's experiences attempt to keep us disconnected from our purpose. Personal transformation brings us back into alignment, where our blueprint comes alive. Transformation happens when we keep stepping forward, one aligned action at a time.

Whether your impact is in your family, your community, or on a global scale, your inner world shapes the outer world. Transformation doesn't just stop at the self. When you heal, you influence others to do the same. Every individual who expands their awareness, intentionally shifting from reaction to co-creation, contributes to a greater collective shift.

Quantum Leadership is the energetic shift in self and the systems we influence.

A new world is built, one choice at a time.

My first-grade teacher gave me two incredible gifts: a love for leadership and an understanding that the system is what we make it. In our little classroom town, she made it clear we could choose to create something new. And now, at scale, it's time for us to do the same. It's time to remake our systems, beginning with ourselves and extending into our communities, our businesses, and the collective.

It starts within. It starts with you.

**If you want to change your life, change your choices.**

Recognize where you are out of sync with your inner system, reassess what is depleting and what is restoring, and rebuild your daily life around sustainable progress in the right direction. Recalibrating fragmentation is all about returning to your inherent wholeness—for yourself and collective benefit.

Quantum principles teach us that everything—thoughts, emotions, actions—is energy, and that energy ripples through the field, shaping what we experience and what our sphere of influence experiences.

With Energetic Intelligence, you attune to and act from Inner Authority—aligning with your blueprint, the unique expression of your purpose that flows through Quantum Intelligence into how you live, lead, and influence the world.

Transformation is not just about what we overcome. It's about what we do with what we've learned. You can spend years healing, searching, excavating. But the real shift begins when you can move from asking, "what happened to me" to "how can I use my experiences to help others?"

If this book has offered you anything, let it be that your personal growth is inseparable from the world you want to help create. Your *transformation* is your *leadership*.

Whether you are a leader in business, an activist shaping social change, or an individual committed to living with greater purpose and fulfillment, this is your invitation to integrate everything you've learned into your daily life—to share your healing.

Imagine the impact if *one billion* people were to choose alignment over fear, clarity over confusion, healing over survival.

---

## THE COLLECTIVE REVOLUTION IS DEEPLY PERSONAL. REAL CHANGE DOESN'T START WITH INSTITUTIONS OR POLICIES; IT STARTS WITH PEOPLE WHO CHOOSE TO LEAD DIFFERENTLY.

---

Leadership is not a fixed state. It is an evolving process that mirrors both personal growth and societal progression. We are not static beings, nor do we exist in isolation. Just as individuals move through stages of contraction and expansion, so too do cultures, systems, and entire civilizations.

One step at a time.

One moment at a time.

**Collective transformation doesn't just happen; it's something we co-create.**

*The Quantum Blueprint* is not a rigid formula but a roadmap for conscious personal and collective leadership in action. One that will challenge you, stretch you, and ultimately elevate not only your own life but the world around you.

This book has given you a framework for personal and collective transformation, but frameworks mean nothing without action. Growth and transformation aren't waiting for the perfect moment. *It's happening right now*, in the life you already have, *unfolding in the choices you make every day*—in small, deliberate shifts.

This book was never about just healing; it's about self-leadership, stepping fully into your power, and embodying the life you were always meant to live.

You've done the deep work. You've repaired fragmentation, reclaimed your energy, and remembered who you really are. Now bring that inner alignment into every conversation, every choice, every space you touch. Put your blueprint into motion—your personal code for leading yourself and shaping the world through the way you live and lead.

The next chapter of your life begins the moment you decide to start living it.

You are not here to wait for permission. You are not here to play small. You are here to live your blueprint—to lead from the wholeness you fought to embody, and to witness that integrity flowing through every room, every system, and every life you touch.

The world needs *activated leaders*—your calling starts now.

This is *our* zero point.

**You are the blueprint.**

**Activation**

**Inquiry**

**INTEGRATION**
**INNER AUTHORITY**
**EMBODIMENT**

**Alignment**

**FOR POSITIVE COLLECTIVE IMPACT**

# QUANTUM BLUEPRINT

**Activating Blueprint:** The Quantum Blueprint is your unique gift, purpose, and calling in this moment in time. When intention meets integrity, personal transformation amplifies into collective impact—Quantum Strategy invites you to use activation and inquiry to align with your collective purpose—bridging personal evolution with collective transformation.

## ACTIVATING YOUR BLUEPRINT

The ALIGNED pillars move from concept into practice across six stages—from activation to collective impact. Each one moves you closer to personal integrity, energetic coherence, and conscious leadership. It always begins with a moment of activation—an internal or external disruption that invites pause and reflection, returning you to the zero point, where your response influences the outcome.

### STAGE 1: ACTIVATION

This is the spark—the recognition of misalignment. You feel off, reactive, emotionally overwhelmed, or like something isn't working anymore. There is felt tension in your body, relationships, or environment.

**Energetic cue:** Something *feels* off; energy is fragmented.

**Reflection:** What part of me is activated? What is this inviting me to examine?

### STAGE 2: INQUIRY

Rather than reacting, you turn inward with curiosity. This is where you separate fragmentated identity from your true self. Observe without judgment to release stagnant energy.

**Energetic cue:** Overidentified with fear, expectation, or old patterns.

**Reflection:** What part of me is speaking? Is this my authentic self, or a protective part? What fear or belief is underneath this response? How do I want to respond?

## STAGE 3: INTEGRATION

Now that you've met the activated part, invite it into recalibration. Acknowledge the wisdom of your protective patterns, then choose to lead from Inner Authority instead.

**Energetic cue:** A softening, remembering who you are beyond the wound.

**Practice:** Scripting, EFT tapping, dialoguing with the part, affirming safety.

## STAGE 4: INNER AUTHORITY

You've reached a grounded sense of clarity and integrity that guides choices and actions even in moments of pressure. Refine through repetition, discerning what is aligned, sustainable, purposeful, and yours to carry. Release roles, responsibilities, or stories that no longer serve your mission for collective regeneration.

**Energetic cue:** Confidence without force. Choices feel spacious, steady, and directed.

**Practice:** Act from clarity—own your values, trust your discernment, and stand firm in aligned decisions.

## STAGE 5: EMBODIMENT

Begin translating inner work into aligned action—choices match your healed values, identity, and Inner Authority. Let coherence guide how you show up, speak, or set boundaries.

**Energetic cue:** Calm clarity—energy and values are moving in the same direction.

**Practice:** Choose the next step based on coherence; trust the body's "yes."

## STAGE 6: COLLECTIVE IMPACT

Embodied alignment creates coherence—coherence entrains; the system shifts. Become aware of the impact you carry, and consciously choose how it ripples into the collective—to transform teams, heal families, and support community flourishing.

**Energetic cue:** Your presence empowers others.

**Practice:** Lead by example. Be the catalyst. Align first and influence through resonance.

**SOULUTIONS**

You began this book with the goal of unlocking your personal power, leading with integrity, and fulfilling your purpose. Now you have the map: EnQ to sense, Quantum Strategy to decide, ALIGNED to move.

As you activate your blueprint, these questions will keep you grounded and in motion. Return to them often, or when friction arises, as guideposts and reflection prompts to recalibrate.

**CHAPTER 1 SOULUTIONS**

1. Where might unhealed patterns or unconscious behaviors be leaking through your current leadership style?
2. When conflict or stress arises, what sensations show up in your body—and what might they be trying to reveal?
3. If your leadership were a transmission of wholeness, how would it feel to lead from full integrity?

**CHAPTER 2 SOULUTIONS**

1. What personal experiences most shaped how you view power, success, and responsibility?
2. What past experiences still influence your reactions today—and how might you respond differently now?
3. How might your past be a key to unlocking your unique gift for others?

**CHAPTER 3 SOULUTIONS**

1. What messages did you absorb growing up about what a "good leader" looks like, and how do those messages shape your leadership today?
2. In what ways does your current lifestyle support or sabotage your ability to lead from coherence?

3. What would it look like if your leadership flowed from your fully healed and integrated self?

## CHAPTER 4 SOULUTIONS

1. Where do you notice tension between your actions and your values, and what opportunity might that reveal?
2. In moments of friction, where do you feel constriction, avoidance, or intensity, and what new awareness might it be pointing to?
3. What's happening in your body in these moments? What does alignment feel like in your body? What does misalignment feel like?

## CHAPTER 5 SOULUTIONS

1. What emotions am I feeling? What pattern is repeating? What belief is being reinforced? What do I choose to believe instead?
2. When do you notice yourself choosing control over flow, and what does that show you?
3. What would it mean for you to trust the field—to co-create with Quantum Intelligence?

## CHAPTER 6 SOULUTIONS

1. What emerges when you lead from regulated coherence rather than fear, survival, or chaos?
2. How do people and environments respond to your presence?
3. What kind of legacy do you want to leave—and how might aligned leadership be the doorway?

## CHAPTER 7 SOULUTIONS

1. If you're no longer living to prove, what possibility are you now willing to see?
2. Where have you outsourced your authority to people, systems, or fear?
3. What does *yes* feel like in your body? What does *no* feel like? What would your life look like if you fully trusted yourself?

## CHAPTER 8 SOULUTIONS

1. What narratives or distortions cloud your ability to connect with your inner knowing?
2. When do you feel most attuned to subtle cues, intuition, or energetic clarity?
3. What would be possible if you consistently operated from Energetic Intelligence?

## CHAPTER 9 SOULUTIONS

1. What patterns do you notice repeating in your relationships—especially under pressure?
2. Where does tension show up when you try to remain "right," "safe," or "in control"?
3. In what ways do your relationships offer opportunities for you to grow?

## CHAPTER 10 SOULUTIONS

1. What might reflect someone else's version of success—and what feels truly aligned for *you*?
2. What is the cost of not acting on this? And what could be possible if you took aligned action?
3. What signals do you typically trust, and which do you dismiss? When have you trusted your inner guidance, what happened?

**CHAPTER 11 SOULUTIONS**

1. What is the single most transformative insight this book has activated for you so far?
2. What aligned action are you now being called to take?
3. Who are you becoming, and what is one step that would support you in honoring that version today?

**CHAPTER 12 SOULUTIONS**

1. How do your daily choices shape the collective systems you're a part of?
2. What signal does your energy carry when you enter a room or a conversation?
3. What kind of world do you believe is possible—and how can you help co-create it?

**CHAPTER 13 SOULUTIONS**

1. What support, structure, or community do you need to stay aligned with your transformation?
2. Where are you being invited to reclaim power you once outsourced—energetically, emotionally, or systemically?
3. What deeper calling or vision is now undeniable?

**YOUR QUANTUM BLUEPRINT**

1. What is *your* definition of success, and how will you embody it?
2. What energy are you amplifying through your choices, and how is it shaping those around you?
3. What lasting imprint do you want your leadership to leave on the collective?

# AFTERWORD

I don't claim to embody or to have perfected Quantum Leadership. I emphasize it because I've experienced the difference it makes, and I know it's what our world desperately needs. I don't hold myself above any of the leaders or teams I've described. I've stumbled, made mistakes, and navigated my way forward just as they have. They key differentiator is to keep turning toward transformation, even when it's uncomfortable.

In hindsight, I've realized the "Blink" sections mirror parts work—revisiting each age, each wound, allowing the energy of those moments to exist in safety and coherence in the present.

I couldn't control what I went through or change what I once accepted, but the moment I became conscious of the systemic forces hurting us all, it was no longer possible to ignore injustice, enable extractive systems, or allow mistreatment in any form—whether in friendship, work, or community. That doesn't mean I am perfect or above mistakes; it means I am committed to evolving and integrating each lesson into who I am becoming.

The work of personal transformation, energetics, and Quantum Leadership is to integrate the fragments of who we've been so we can become whole and of service, in our unique purpose.

Your life is waiting for you to claim it.

You are not broken. You are not behind. You are not too late.

You don't need permission. Stop waiting for certainty or the perfect moment.

The moment is now.

Heal. Live.

Whatever dreams have been placed on your heart are there for a reason.

Step into everything you were always meant to be.

Your healing matters. Your evolution matters.

The world is waiting for *you*.

Your light—your unique, irreplaceable, powerful presence—matters.

Step in. Even if it's messy. Even if it's uncertain. Even if you don't know where it's leading.

*Meet me in the water.*

The current will carry you where you need to go.

The choice is yours. Stay comfortable or step up.

Let the old world continue or be part of creating a new one.

This book invites you to navigate the process of personal transformation in pursuit of collective evolution—a shared commitment to growth. My hope is that you will test these ideas in your own life and leadership, bringing forth possibilities only realized together.

You have the power to change more than just your life.

You have the power to change the future—for yourself and others.

What will you do with it?

# GLOSSARY

**Abundance:** The availability of what you need, when you need it, to fulfill your purpose—spiritually, emotionally, energetically, or materially.

**Activation:** Emotional or energetic responses (often uncomfortable) that signal misalignment; invitations for healing, reflection, or recalibration; a starting point for deeper self-inquiry and growth.

**ALIGNED™:** The practical arc from misalignment to personal mastery: Awareness → Leadership → Intentionality → Growth → Embodiment → Discernment.

**Alignment:** The state of being in conscious connection with your values, truth, and source energy—measured not by intention but by how often you act in accordance with it. Frequency matters.

**Clarity (energetic congruence):** A felt sense of internal alignment, unclouded by past wounds, trauma filters, or collective programming—how you perceive. A perceptual state of clean, unclouded awareness, free from distortion by trauma, social conditioning, or survival patterns. Clarity reflects your inner truth as you experience it, even if it differs from others. It is the foundation for energetic discernment and Inner Authority.

**Coherence:** A state where your thoughts, emotions, actions, and energetic frequency are in alignment, allowing you to move through the world in integrity with your Inner Authority—producing clarity, integrity, and trustworthy leadership.

**Energetic Imprint:** The underlying code or pattern of your vibrational state, reflecting both your wounds and your wisdom, and determining how energy flows through you.

**Energetic Intelligence (EnQ):** The ability to sense, interpret, and influence the energy in yourself and others to create aligned, coherent, and transformational impact—personally, interpersonally, and systemically.

**Energetic Recalibration:** The intentional process of resetting your internal frequency from survival, suppression, or fragmentation into alignment and coherence.

**Faith:** Trusting unseen resonance.

**Field:** The relational or organizational energetic environment; *signals* are the patterns (data, behavior, emotion, results) that reveal coherence or friction in the field.

**Fragmentation:** The experience of being disconnected from your core self, often as a protective response to trauma or systemic misalignment.

**Frequency/Vibration:** The quality of energy you are embodying or transmitting—what others feel before they understand you.

**Inner Authority:** The felt sense that arises when you are in clarity and coherence. It bypasses external validation or inherited systems of control, enabling action rooted in self-honoring awareness.

**Inner Guidance System:** The body's sensory and regulatory network, including the nervous system, fascia, and biomagnetic field. This system detects and interprets signals from our inner and outer environments, guiding us toward alignment, safety, and optimal performance.

**Integration:** The process of reclaiming and reintegrating disowned or traumatized parts of the self—allowing for greater coherence and energetic alignment.

**Interconnectedness:** The reality that all things—energetically and systemically—are influencing one another at all times.

**Internal Operating System:** The integrated network of mind, body, and soul that governs how we think, feel, act, and relate to the world. Alignment of this system creates coherence across all aspects of our being.

**Mental Fitness:** The capacity to observe, regulate, and redirect thoughts and emotional patterns in real time. Mental fitness strengthens the neural pathways needed for clarity, discernment, and presence—forming the cognitive foundation for interpreting energetic signals and embodying aligned leadership.

**Misalignment:** A state of energetic dissonance between what you know, feel, or value and how you show up or lead.

**Nervous System Regulation:** The ability to maintain or restore calm, safety, and connection in the body—critical for leading with presence and responsiveness rather than reactivity.

**Personal Transformation:** The process of returning to wholeness by reclaiming suppressed truth, healing disconnection, and leading from energetic alignment.

**Quantum Blueprint:** Your unique energetic pattern—shaped by your lived experience, Inner Authority, and soul path—that guides how you lead, love, and impact the world when fully aligned.

**Quantum Intelligence:** (1) All-knowing intelligence, accessible beyond time, mind, and matter—reflecting your capacity to lead through presence, energetic awareness, coherence, and multidimensional alignment. (2) The universal, collective intelligence of the quantum field. Represents the source of interconnected information and energy that shapes potential and possibility. While it is constant and universal, our ability to perceive and apply it varies.

**Quantum Leadership:** (1) Leadership that moves beyond personal achievement to systems healing and human-centered impact. (2) Leading from energetic coherence—aligning intention, attention, and action—toward positive collective impact so systems entrain toward integrity and exponential results.

**Quantum Strategy:** A discipline designed to generate human-centered, positive collective impact by aligning vision, energy, and execution to collapse time between intention and outcome.

**Resonance:** (1) The natural harmony between two or more frequencies. (2) The felt sense of alignment, when your internal frequency matches the field—experienced through tone, body language, presence, or timing. When shared, resonance creates energetic amplification, magnifying presence, trust, and clarity.

**Shadow:** Any part of the self that has been suppressed, rejected, or exiled—often unconsciously—and that unconsciously drives behavior until integrated.

**Signal:** Present sensed and observable patterns (data, behavior, emotion, results) that reveal coherence or friction.

**Sphere of Influence:** Any network, organization, or group in which your energy, leadership, or presence alters behavior or culture.

**Systemic Fragmentation:** The organizational or societal by-product of unhealed leadership—resulting in incoherence, burnout, or harm to human dignity.

**Toxic Positivity:** The denial or dismissal of authentic emotions—particularly pain, grief, fear, or doubt—under the pressure to "stay positive" or appear unaffected.

**Traditional/Industrial Leadership:** Leadership centered around control, performance, hierarchy, and external authority.

**Trauma:** Any experience—acute or cumulative—that exceeds your capacity to process, integrate, or make meaning of it in the moment (or shortly after).

**Truth:** (1) Your unique experience, perspective, perception, and lived experience. (2) Your character, values, purpose, perception, and perspective.

**Zero Point:** The baseline of all potential—a still, charged state beneath form, between stimulus and response, where aligned choice creates exponential impact.

# RESOURCES

**Influential Works and Supporting Research:** In addition to the footnotes, the following list of books, studies, and creative works shared here shaped my learning, challenged my perspective, or illuminated new pathways along the way. Many great thinkers, writers, and practitioners have contributed to this field. They've helped inform my personal transformation and the insights, framework, and vision for *The Quantum Blueprint*.

### PSYCHOLOGY, LEADERSHIP, AND ORGANIZATION DEVELOPMENT

- Margaret J. Wheatley, *Leadership and the New Science: Discovering Order in a Chaotic World* (Berrett-Koehler, 1992).
- Margaret J. Wheatley, *Who Do We Choose to Be? Facing Reality, Claiming Leadership, Restoring Sanity* (Berrett-Koehler, 2017).
- C. Otto Scharmer, *Theory U: Leading from the Future as It Emerges* (Society for Organizational Learning, 2007).
- Sandra L. Bem, "Gender Schema Theory: A Cognitive Account of Sex Typing," *Psychological Review* 88, no. 4 (1981): 354–64.

- Stephen W. Porges, *The Polyvagal Theory: Neurophysiological Foundations of Emotions, Attachment, Communication, and Self-Regulation* (W. W. Norton, 2011).
- Daniel Goleman, *Working with Emotional Intelligence* (Bantam Books, 1998).
- Amy C. Edmondson, *The Fearless Organization: Creating Psychological Safety in the Workplace for Learning, Innovation, and Growth* (John Wiley & Sons, 2018).
- Robert Kegan, *In Over Our Heads: The Mental Demands of Modern Life* (Harvard University Press, 1994).
- Robert Kegan and Lisa Laskow Lahey, *How the Way We Talk Can Change the Way We Work: Seven Languages for Transformation* (Jossey-Bass, 2000).
- Robert Kegan and Lisa Laskow Lahey, *Immunity to Change: How to Overcome It and Unlock the Potential in Yourself and Your Organization* (Harvard Business Press, 2009).
- Norman Doidge, *The Brain That Changes Itself: Stories of Personal Triumph from the Frontiers of Brain Science* (Viking, 2007).
- Donald L. Anderson, *Organization Development: The Process of Leading Organizational Change*, 5th ed. (SAGE Publications, 2020).
- W. Warner Burke, *Organization Change: Theory and Practice*, 3rd ed. (SAGE Publications, 2010).
- Virginia Anderson and Lauren Johnson, *Systems Thinking Basics: From Concepts to Causal Loops* (Pegasus Communications, 1997).
- Chris Crosby, *Strategic Organizational Alignment: Authority, Power, Results* (Business Expert Press, 2020).
- James M. Kouzes and Barry Z. Posner, *The Leadership Challenge*, 6th ed. (ohn Wiley & Sons, 2017).
- Jim Dethmer, Diana Chapman, and Kaley Klemp, *The 15 Commitments of Conscious Leadership* (Dethmer, Chapman & Klemp, 2015).
- Lee G. Bolman and Terrence E. Deal, *Reframing Organizations: Artistry, Choice, and Leadership*, 6th ed. (Jossey-Bass, 2017).

- Peter G. Northouse, *Leadership: Theory and Practice*, 9th ed. (SAGE Publications, 2021).
- The Arbinger Institute, *Leadership and Self-Deception*, 2nd ed. (Berrett-Koehler Publishers, 2010).
- Craig E. Johnson, *Organizational Ethics: A Practical Approach*, 4th ed. (SAGE Publications, 2015).
- Arthur A. Thompson, Margaret A. Peteraf, John E. Gamble, and A. J. Strickland, *Crafting and Executing Strategy: The Quest for Competitive Advantage*, 20th ed. (McGraw-Hill Education, 2016).

**ENERGETICS, HEALING, AND HUMAN POTENTIAL**

- Rollin McCraty, Mike Atkinson, William A. Tiller, Glen Rein, and Alan D. Watkins, "The Effects of Emotions on Short-Term Power Spectrum Analysis of Heart Rate Variability," *American Journal of Cardiology* 76, no. 14 (1995): 1089–93.
- Rollin McCraty, Mike Atkinson, Dana Tomasino, and Raymond Trevor Bradley, "The Coherent Heart: Heart-Brain Interactions, Psychophysiological Coherence, and the Emergence of System-Wide Order," Publication No. 06-022 (Boulder Creek, CA: HeartMath Research Center, Institute of HeartMath, 2006).
- Kacey Cardin, "Leading with Energetic Intelligence," TEDx Talk, 2020, video.
- Lisa Feldman Barrett, *How Emotions Are Made: The Secret Life of the Brain* (Houghton Mifflin Harcourt, 2017).
- Stephen W. Porges, *The Polyvagal Theory: Neurophysiological Foundations of Emotions, Attachment, Communication, and Self-Regulation* (W. W. Norton, 2011).
- Joe Dispenza, *Becoming Supernatural: How Common People Are Doing the Uncommon* (Hay House, 2017).
- Bruce Lipton, *The Biology of Belief: Unleashing the Power of Consciousness, Matter & Miracles* (Hay House, 2005).

- Michael J. Meaney, "Epigenetics and Maternal Care: Nature versus Nurture," *American Journal of Psychiatry* 161, no. 9 (2004): 1630–32.
- Deepak Chopra, *Metahuman: Unleashing Your Infinite Potential* (Harmony Books, 2019).
- Deepak Chopra, *Abundance: The Inner Path to Wealth* (Harmony Books, 2022).
- Bruce D. Perry and Oprah Winfrey, *What Happened to You?: Conversations on Trauma, Resilience, and Healing* (Flatiron Books, 2021).
- Athena Perrakis, *The Ultimate Guide to Chakras: The Beginner's Guide to Balancing, Healing, and Unblocking Your Chakras for Health and Positive Energy* (Fair Winds Press, 2018).
- David Filipe, *Reiki Healing for Beginners: Unlocking the Secrets of Aura Cleansing, Chakra Healing, and Energy Healing* (self-pub., 2020).
- Michael Newton, *Journey of Souls: Case Studies of Life between Lives* (Llewellyn Publications, 1994).
- Thich Nhat Hanh, *How to Practice: The Way to a Meaningful Life* (Parallax Press, 2002).
- Thich Nhat Hanh, *The Heart of the Buddha's Teaching: Transforming Suffering into Peace, Joy, and Liberation* (Broadway Books, 1998).
- Thich Nhat Hanh, *Anger: Wisdom for Cooling the Flames* (Riverhead Books, 2001).
- Thich Nhat Hanh, *The Art of Communicating* (HarperOne, 2013).
- Thich Nhat Hanh, *No Mud, No Lotus: The Art of Transforming Suffering* (Parallax Press, 2014).
- Thich Nhat Hanh, *Reconciliation: Healing the Inner Child* (Parallax Press, 2010).
- Colin Tipping, *Radical Forgiveness: A Revolutionary Five-Stage Process to Heal Relationships, Let Go of Anger and Blame, and Find Peace in Any Situation*, 2nd ed. (Sounds True, 2010).
- Michael Bernard Beckwith, *Life Visioning: A Transformative*

*Process for Activating Your Unique Gifts and Highest Potential* (Sounds True, 2011).
- Parker J. Palmer, *A Hidden Wholeness: The Journey toward an Undivided Life* (Jossey-Bass, 2004).
- Malcolm Gladwell, *Outliers: The Story of Success* (Little, Brown, 2008).
- Vishen Lakhiani, *The Code of the Extraordinary Mind: 10 Unconventional Laws to Redefine Your Life and Succeed on Your Own Terms* (Rodale Books, 2016).
- David R. Hawkins, *Power vs. Force: The Hidden Determinants of Human Behavior* (Hay House, 1995).Quantum, Philosophical, and Interdisciplinary Thought
- Richard Feynman, *Six Easy Pieces: Essentials of Physics Explained by Its Most Brilliant Teacher* (Basic Books, 1994).
- Richard Feynman, *Six Not-So-Easy Pieces: Einstein's Relativity, Symmetry, and Space-Time* (Basic Books, 1997).
- Peter J. Lewis, *Quantum Ontology: A Guide to the Metaphysics of Quantum Mechanics* (Oxford University Press, 2016).
- Immanuel Kant, *Critique of Practical Reason*, trans. Mary Gregor (Cambridge University Press, 1788/1997).
- Max Tegmark, *Life 3.0: Being Human in the Age of Artificial Intelligence* (Alfred A. Knopf, 2017).
- Jim Holt, *When Einstein Walked with Gödel: Excursions to the Edge of Thought* (Farrar, Straus and Giroux, 2018).
- Viktor Frankl, *The Will to Meaning: Foundations and Applications of Logotherapy* (New American Library, 1988/1969).
- Marcus Aurelius, *Meditations*, trans. Gregory Hays (Modern Library, 2006).
- Steven Pressfield, *The Warrior Ethos* (Black Irish Entertainment, 2011).
- Frédéric Lenoir, *Happiness: A Philosopher's Guide*, trans. Andrew Brown (Melville House, 2015).
- Jonathan Haidt, *The Happiness Hypothesis: Finding Modern Truth in Ancient Wisdom* (Basic Books, 2006).

- Cam Kam Knight, *Mind Mapping: Improve Memory, Concentration, Communication, Organization, Creativity, and Time Management* (CreateSpace, 2013/2012).

**NEUROSCIENCE AND PSYCHOLOGY**

- Bryan Kolb and Ian Q. Whishaw, *Fundamentals of Human Neuropsychology*, 3rd ed. (W. H. Freeman, 1995).
- Mark F. Bear, Barry W. Connors, and Michael A. Paradiso, *Neuroscience: Exploring the Brain*, 4th ed. (Wolters Kluwer, 2015).
- Ronald E. Riggio, *Introduction to Industrial/Organizational Psychology*, 7th ed. (Pearson, 2012).
- Arielle Schwartz and Barbara Maiberger, *EMDR Therapy and Somatic Psychology: Interventions to Enhance Embodiment in Trauma Treatment* (W. W. Norton, 2018).
- John Beebe, *Energies and Patterns in Psychological Type* (Routledge, 2016/2017).
- Gillian Butler, Nick Grey, and Tony Hope, *Managing Your Mind: The Mental Fitness Guide*, 3rd ed. (Oxford University Press, 2018).
- Albert Ellis, *How to Control Your Anxiety Before It Controls You* (Citadel Press, 1997).

**CULTURAL INFLUENCES AND ART**

- *Everything Everywhere All at Once* (film, 2022).
- *Final Destination* (film, 2000).

**CONSCIOUS CAPITALISM AND ECONOMIC SYSTEMS DEVELOPMENT**

- John Mackey and Raj Sisodia, *Conscious Capitalism* (Harvard Business Review Press, 2013).

# NOTES

1. *Psychological Safety and Learning Behavior in Work Teams.* Administrative Science Quarterly, 44(2), 350–383.

2. Manfred F. R. Kets de Vries, *The Leader on the Couch: A Clinical Approach to Changing People and Organizations* (Jossey-Bass, 2006).

3. Paul Babiak and Robert D. Hare, *Snakes in Suits: When Psychopaths Go to Work* (Harper, 2006).

4. Jeffrey Pfeffer, *Dying for a Paycheck: How Modern Management Harms Employee Health and Company Performance—and What We Can Do about It* (HarperBusiness, 2018).

5. James MacGregor Burns, *Leadership* (Harper Torchbooks, 1978) and *Transforming Leadership* (Grove Press, 2004).

6. Daniel Goleman et al., *Primal Leadership: Realizing the Power of Emotional Intelligence* (Harvard Business School Press, 2002).

7. Bernard M. Bass, *Leadership and Performance Beyond Expectations* (Free Press, 1985).

8. EnQ® is a registered trademark of Kacey Cardin. I use the term in this book to describe my own distinct body of work and lived understanding of Energetic Intelligence, grounded in Quantum Leadership and Organization Development.

9. Rachel Yehuda and Amy Lehrner, "Intergenerational Transmission of Trauma Effects: Putative Role of Epigenetic Mechanisms," World Psychiatry 17, no. 3 (2018): 243–57.

10. Peter A. Levine, *Waking the Tiger: Healing Trauma* (North Atlantic Books, 1997).

11. Nadine Burke Harris, *The Deepest Well: Healing the Long-Term Effects of Childhood Adversity* (Houghton Mifflin Harcourt, 2018).

12. Vincent J. Felitti et al., "Relationship of Childhood Abuse and Household Dysfunction to Many of the Leading Causes of Death in Adults: The Adverse Childhood Experiences (ACE) Study," American Journal of Preventive Medicine 14, no. 4 (1998): 245–58; Yehuda and Lehrner, "Intergenerational Transmission of Trauma Effects, *World Psychiatry* 17, no. 3 (2018): 243–57.

13. Rick Hanson and Richard Mendius, Buddha's Brain: The Practical Neuroscience of Happiness, Love & Wisdom (New Harbinger Publications, 2009).

14. G. A. Bonanno, "Loss, Trauma, and Human Resilience: Have We Underestimated the Human Capacity to Thrive After Extremely Aversive Events?," American Psychologist 59, no. 1 (2004): 20–28.

15. Judith Herman, Trauma and Recovery (Basic Books, 1992).

16. Bessel van der Kolk, *The Body Keeps the Score: Brain, Mind, and Body in the Healing of Trauma* (Penguin Books, 2014).

17. Christina Maslach and Michael P. Leiter, "Understanding the Burnout Experience: Recent Research and Its Implications for Psychiatry," World Psychiatry 15, no. 2 (2016): 103–11.

18. Dacher Keltner, *The Power Paradox: How We Gain and Lose Influence* (Penguin Books, 2016).

19. SHRM, The High Cost of a Toxic Workplace Culture (SHRM, 2019).

20. David Graeber, Bullshit Jobs: A Theory (Simon & Schuster, 2019).

21. Richard J. Davidson and Sharon Begley, *The Emotional Life of Your Brain: How Its Unique Patterns Affect the Way You Think, Feel, and Live—and How You Can Change Them* (Avery, 2012); Daniel J. Siegel, *The Developing Mind: How Relationships and the Brain Interact to Shape Who We Are*, 2nd ed. (Guilford Press, 2012).

22. Brené Brown, Dare to Lead: Brave Work. Tough Conversations. Whole Hearts (Random House, 2018).

23. Gabor Maté, When the Body Says No: Understanding the Stress-Disease Connection (John Wiley & Sons, 2003).

24. Jeffrey M. Schwartz and Sharon Begley, The Mind and the Brain: Neuroplasticity and the Power of Mental Force (ReganBooks, 2002).

25. Carl Jung, The Archetypes and the Collective Unconscious (Princeton University Press, 1981); Sam Harris, *Waking Up: A Guide to Spirituality Without Religion* (Simon & Schuster Paperbacks, 2014).

26. Herbert Benson, The Relaxation Response (HarperTorch, 2000); and Andrew Newberg, *How God Changes Your Brain: Breakthrough Findings from a Leading Neuroscientist* (Ballantine, 2009).

27. Michael A. Singer, The Surrender Experiment (Harmony, 2015).

28. Rosabeth Moss Kanter, *Men and Women of the Corporation* (Basic Books, 1993).

29. Alice H. Eagly and Steven J. Karau, "Role Congruity Theory of Prejudice toward Female Leaders," Psychological Review 109, no. 3 (2002): 573–98.

30. Alice H. Eagly and Wendy Wood, "Social Role Theory," in Handbook of Theories of Social Psychology, eds. Paul A. M. Van Lange, Arie W. Kruglanski, and E. Tory Higgins, vol. 2 (Sage Publications, 2012), 458–76.

31  Sandra Bem, "Gender Schema Theory: A Cognitive Account of Sex Typing." Psychological Review, no. 4 (1981): 354-364.

32  Rutger Bregman, Humankind (Little, Brown, 2019); Mariana Mazzucato, The Value of Everything (PublicAffairs, 2018); Kate Raworth, Doughnut Economics: 7 Ways to Think Like a 21st Century Economist (Chelsea Green Publishing, 2017) and A Safe and Just Space for Humanity (Oxfam Discussion Papers, February 2012); Robert D. Putnam, "Bowling Alone: America's Declining Social Capital," Journal of Democracy 6, no. 1 (1995): 65–78 and Bowling Alone: The Collapse and Revival of American Community (Simon & Schuster Paperbacks, 2000).

33  Frederic Laloux, Reinventing Organizations (Nelson Parker, 2014).

34  Shoshana Zuboff, The Age of Surveillance Capitalism (PublicAffairs, 2019).

35  Edward S. Herman and Noam Chomsky, Manufacturing Consent: The Political Economy of the Mass Media (Pantheon Books, 2002).

36  Carl Rogers, On Becoming a Person (Houghton Mifflin Company, 1961); Carl Rogers, A Way of Being (Houghton Mifflin Company, 1980).

37  Adam Grant, Originals: How Non-Conformists Move the World (Penguin Books, 2016); Cass R. Sunstein, *Why Societies Need Dissent* (Harvard University Press, 2005); Cass R. Sunstein and Reid Hastie, *Wiser: Getting Beyond Groupthink to Make Groups Smarter* (Harvard Business Review Press, 2015).

38  Gallup, State of the Global Workplace: 2023 Report (Gallup, Inc., 2023).

39  Richard C. Schwartz, Internal Family Systems Therapy, 2nd ed. (Guilford Press, 2021).

40  Robert A. Johnson, Owning Your Own Shadow: Understanding the Dark Side of the Psyche (HarperCollins, 1991).

41  Alice Miller, The Drama of the Gifted Child: The Search for the True Self, rev. ed. (Basic Books, 1997); Carl G. Jung, Psychological Types, trans. H. G. Baynes, rev. ed., by R. F. C. Hull (Princeton University Press, 1971; originally published 1921).

42  Robert Kegan, The Evolving Self: Problem and Process in Human Development (Harvard University Press, 1982).

43  Andy Jassy, "2024 Letter to Shareholders," Amazon.com, Inc., April 10, 2025.

44  Daniel Goleman, Emotional Intelligence: Why It Can Matter More Than IQ (Bantam Books, 1995).

45  Rollin McCraty, *Science of the Heart, Volume 2: Exploring the Role of the Heart in Human Performance* (Boulder Creek, CA: HeartMath Institute, 2015).

46  Harville Hendrix, Getting the Love You Want: A Guide for Couples (Henry Holt, 1988); John M. Gottman and Nan Silver, The Seven Principles for Making Marriage Work (Harmony, 1999); John M. Gottman, The Science of Trust: Emotional Attunement for Couples (W. W. Norton, 2011).

47  Joseph Luft and Harrington Ingham, "The Johari Window: A Graphic Model of Interpersonal Awareness." presented at the Western Training Laboratory in Group Development (UCLA/NTL) in July 1955; Joseph Luft, Of Human Interaction (Mayfield Publishing, 1969).

48  Charles Handy, The Empty Raincoat: Making Sense of the Future (Arrow, 1995) and *Understanding Organizations* (Oxford University Press, 1993).

49  Kurt Lewin, Principles of Topological Psychology (McGraw-Hill, 1936); and "Frontiers in Group Dynamics: Concept, Method and Reality in Social Science; Social Equilibria and Social Change," Human Relations 1, no. 1 (1947): 5–41; Bernard Burnes, "Kurt Lewin and the Planned Approach to Change: A Re-Appraisal," Journal of Management Studies 41, no. 6 (2004): 977–1002.

50  Abraham H. Maslow, "A Theory of Human Motivation," Psychological Review 50, no. 4 (1943): 370–96; Leroy Little Bear, "Jagged Worldviews Colliding," in Reclaiming Indigenous Voice and Vision, ed. Marie Battiste (University of British Columbia Press, 2000), 77–85; Cindy Blackstock, "The Emergence of the Breath of Life Theory," Journal of Social Work Values and Ethics 8, no. 1 (2011): 1–16.

51  Christopher Lasch, The Culture of Narcissism: American Life in an Age of Diminishing Expectations (W. W. Norton, 2018).

52  Richard Sennett, The Corrosion of Character (W. W. Norton, 1998).

53  Ayelet Fishbach, Get It Done: Surprising Lessons from the Science of Motivation (Little, Brown Spark, 2022).

54  David Bohm, Wholeness and the Implicate Order (Routledge & Kegan Paul, 1980) and Science, Order, and Creativity (with F. David Peat). (Bantam, 1987).

55  Peter M. Senge, The Fifth Discipline: The Art & Practice of the Learning Organization (Currency, 1990).

www.ingramcontent.com/pod-product-compliance
Lightning Source LLC
Chambersburg PA
CBHW030513080526
44586CB00011B/167